The Black Arch... ...

CARNIVAL OF
MONSTERS

By Ian Potter

Published February 2018 by Obverse Books

Cover Design © Cody Schell

Text © Ian Potter, 2018

Range Editors: James Cooray Smith, Philip Purser-Hallard

Ian would like to thank:

The staff of the BBC Written Archive Centre, Mark Ayres, Piers D Britton, David Butler, James Cooray Smith, Kevin Jon Davies, John Dorney, Stuart Douglas, Matthew J Elliott, Paul Ford, Roy Gill, Ian Greaves, Brian Hodgson, Alistair McGown, Richard Molesworth, Jonathan Morris, Andy Murray, Phil Newman, Andrew Pixley, Philip Purser-Hallard, Paul Rhodes, Steve Roberts, David Rolinson, Kenny Smith and Andrew Wooding.

If he could, he'd particularly like to thank Barry Letts and Robert Holmes.

For Helen, the bona palone who Shirnas my Vorging.

Also Available

CONTENTS

OVERVIEW

Serial Title: *Carnival of Monsters*

Writer: Robert Holmes

Director: Barry Letts

Original UK Transmission Dates: 27 January – 18 February 1973

Running Time: Episode 1: 24m 46s

                              Episode 2: 24m 11s

                              Episode 3: 24m 49s

                              Episode 4: 24m 10s

UK Viewing Figures: Episode 1: 9.5 million

                              Episode 2: 9.0 million

                              Episode 3: 9.0 million

                              Episode 4: 9.2 million

Regular Cast: Jon Pertwee (Dr Who), Katy Manning (Jo Grant)

Guest Cast: Tenniel Evans (Major Daly), Ian Marter (John Andrews), Jenny McCracken (Claire Daly), Leslie Dwyer (Vorg), Cheryl Hall (Shirna), Peter Halliday (Pletrac), Michael Wisher (Kalik), Terence Lodge (Orum), Andrew Staines (Captain)

Antagonists: Kalik, Vorg, Humans, Drashigs.

Novelisation: *Doctor Who and the Carnival of Monsters* by Terrance Dicks. **The Target Doctor Who Library** #8.

Sequels and Prequels: *Goth Opera* (novel, 1994), *The Eight Doctors* (novel, 1997), *The Monsters Are Coming!* (stage play, 2010), *Planet of the Drashigs* (audio, 2019).

Responses:

'It's the real beginning of **Doctor Who**: the most significant and influential story in the series. There is no story like *Carnival of Monsters* before *Carnival of Monsters* – gaudy, hilarious, too clever for kids, unashamedly intellectual – afterwards there are tons...'

[Gareth Roberts, *Doctor Who Magazine: The Complete Third Doctor*]

'*Carnival of Monsters* [...] squanders [...] a rather intriguing first episode mystery, with some of the most appalling character, set, and costume design in the era's history [...]. And [...] we have some superb actors wasted in roles that require them to spout awful faux Shakespearean lines from behind splotchy grey makeup and bald caps.'

[Arnold T Blumberg, 'Doctor Who: *Carnival of Monsters* Special Edition DVD Review', IGN]

SYNOPSIS

Episode 1

The notoriously xenophobic planet Inter Minor has recently opened its borders to a limited number of visitors from other worlds, thanks to reforms initiated by its President, Zarb. Among the first arrivals are two Lurman show people, Vorg and Shirna. They hope to make a fortune on the planet, which has hitherto been starved of cultural experiences. They are greeted, if not welcomed, by two senior bureaucrats, Kalik and Orum, who have reluctantly been allocated the job of meeting the aliens, and who are more concerned with an increase in unrest amongst the Inter Minorian servant class, the Functionaries.

The TARDIS, en route to Metebelis 3, arrives on a ship in the Indian Ocean, early on the evening of 4 June 1926. The ship is attacked by a plesiosaurus, a prehistoric marine reptile native to earth, extinct for millions of years by 1926. In the aftermath of the attack, the Doctor and Jo meet ship's passengers Major Daly and his daughter Claire, and Lieutenant Andrews of the ship's company, who decide the time travellers are stowaways and they are subsequently imprisoned in the Major's cabin. On the way there the Doctor notices an anachronistic metal plate on the ship's deck which Andrews does not seem able to see. Once locked in the Major's cabin the Doctor realises that he and Jo are onboard the SS *Bernice*, a ship that disappeared on the very day on which they have arrived.

Pletrac, a third Inter Minorian bureaucrat, and chair of Orum and Kalik's tribunal arrives. The tribunal quickly decides to expel the entertainers and, stalling for time, Vorg presents them with invalid credentials claiming he was invited to the planet by President Zarb personally.

The Doctor and Jo escape from the Major's cabin using Jo's skeleton keys, and the Doctor examines the anachronistic metal plate anew. He decides it can be opened using a magnetic core extractor, and he happens to have one in the TARDIS. The travellers make their way back to the TARDIS through the lounge of the ship, only to discover that the Dalys and Andrews seem to be re-performing the same actions they were engaged in immediately before they met the Doctor and Jo. That they are in a timeloop of some kind is confirmed when the ship is again attacked by a plesiosaurus and the ship's occupants again react with surprise. The Doctor and Jo return to the hold when a gigantic hand reaches into the ship's hold out of nowhere and grasps the TARDIS.

Episode 2

Vorg pulls a piece of bric a brac out of the Miniscope. It is revealed to be the TARDIS. Vorg demonstrates the Miniscope to the tribunal, and they are horrified to discover that the machine contains live specimens living in timelooped miniature environments. These environments include the SS Bernice. As the crew and passengers of the ship begin yet another loop, the Doctor and Jo escape from the SS Bernice into the inner workings of the Miniscope.

Plectrac confirms that Vorg's credentials are forged, and the tribunal decided that the Scope must be destroyed and orders up a large field gun called an Eradicator for this purpose. The weapon is fired at the Miniscope, which appears undamaged, but the tribunal are mollified by their assumption that the Eradicator must have destroyed the life forms within the scope while leaving the machine intact, having only been designed to damage organic molecules (although the paranoid Kalik insists that Vorg is a spy sent to test their planet's defences). The Doctor and Jo emerge from the scope's workings into a swamp landscape, where a giant monster – a Drashig – rises from the ground to loom over them.

Episode 3

The Doctor and Jo escape from the Drashig swamp into an adjacent cave. While there the Doctor deduces the nature of the machine in which they are trapped and reveals that he was instrumental in Miniscopes being banned by the Time Lords. The Doctor and Jo then return to the scope's workings, but are chased by the Drashigs who have now got their scent.

Much of this is observed by Vorg, Shirna and the tribunal. Pletrac, Kalik and Orum are concerned that not only have the specimens within the scope survived, but that this means that their most advance technology – the Eradicator – is unable to deal with them. Kalik and Orum conspire to create a war to unite all classes of Inter Minorian against a common enemy. To that end they attempt to sabotage the Eradicator, hiding a piece of it in Vorg's luggage so he will be blamed. Their hope is that if and when the Drashigs escape from the scope, the incapacitation of the Eradicator will mean destruction will be widespread, and the Inter Minorians will turn away from President Zarb's liberalising regime and install Kalik as leader.

Jo escapes through the Miniscope's workings back to the SS *Bernice*, where she is again imprisoned by Lieutenant Andrews. The miniaturised Doctor, however, emerges from the scope into the spaceport on Inter Minor.

Episode 4

Outside the Scope, the Doctor returns to his proper size. Pletrac orders him destroyed with the Eradicator, but Kalik objects to this on a point of procedure so that the sabotage of the weapon will not yet be revealed. Relieved to find the TARDIS, the Doctor is also appalled to have his suspicions that he was in a Miniscope confirmed, and informs the tribunal that they have permitted the importation and operation of a machine the existence of which is prohibited under intergalactic law. He tells the overwhelmed tribunal that he may be prepared to overlook their crime if he is permitted to rescue his assistant from the machine. Vorg is impressed by the Doctor's front, and assumes him to be a Tellurian showman. Kalik and Orum plant the piece of the eradicator Orum sabotaged in Vorg's bag, so he will take the blame should their actions be discovered. With Vorg's help, and some material from the TARDIS, the Doctor returns to the inside of the Miniscope to rescue Jo, while Orum and Kalik plot for the Drashigs to escape from the Miniscope. Some Drashigs do escape, but only Kalik is killed, thanks to Vorg effecting repairs of the Eradicator with the piece of it that has been planted in his bags, and using the machine on the escaped Drashigs.

The Doctor rescues Jo, and reveals that when linking the Scope to the TARDIS he arranged for its inhabitants to be returned to where they were originally taken from. The Doctor and Jo depart as Vorg demonstrates a variation on the 'Find the Lady' card trick to an obviously duped Pletrac.

1: 'A STREAM OF INCOMPREHENSIBLE BUT OBVIOUSLY REVOLUTIONARY GOBBLEDEYGOOK'[1]

'If anyone decides that **Doctor Who** is an art form its death knell will be sounded. It is good, clean, escapist hokum which is no small thing to be. When it's done well, it is the best thing of its kind around.'

[Robert Holmes][2]

One of the great things about **Doctor Who** is that it is constructed by many hands for many audiences. It was built to entertain viewers of different ages and consequently has to work on several levels at once to engage them all. That gives us a lot to latch on to.

Carnival of Monsters (1973) is a story all about levels, but it's not the vision of an auteur[3] with a single story or underlying message

---

[1] Stage direction from Robert Holmes' script for *Carnival of Monsters* episode 1, quoted by Malcolm Hulke in *Writing for Television in the 70s* (1974), p185.

[2] A quotation from an unidentified fanzine interview presented in Hearn, Marcus, 'Holmes on Holmes' (*Doctor Who Magazine* (DWM) Winter Special 1994, *Robert Holmes: The Grand Master of Doctor Who*), p36.

[3] Auteur theory arises in French film criticism, presenting a film's director as the primary creator of the work, placing him or her above the screenwriter as 'auteur' of the piece ('auteur' being the French form of 'author'). Students of auteur theory often look to find the signature themes and recurrent techniques of a film maker, which can become problematic when looking at mainstream cinema, where the influences on a piece are many and the director is rarely the work's sole controlling figure.

to relay. It's a show full of episodic set pieces having fun with us and with itself that also happens to be a story full of messages.

Once we get into critical analysis of any work of art, we inevitably open ourselves up to the accusation that we're seeing things in the work that 'aren't there'. Our own expectations, prejudices, historical perspectives and personal contexts will always colour our responses and interpretations. I happen to think that's fine. That's viewing for you – you bring yourself to the show. I also make no apology for the fact that the discussion of the programme you're now reading will end up longer than either the programme's script or its novelisation, and will probably take longer to read than the programme takes to view. There's always more in a script than is on the page, more in a production than ends up on screen, and more than one way to reinterpret it in print.

Some of the things I hope to explore in this brief look at *Carnival of Monsters* will be ideas that were quite deliberately placed there by one or more of the show's many creators. Some will be things that may have slipped in without the creators' knowledge. Some will have arisen simply through the circumstances of the production, or the climate of the time. Others are perhaps more visible now than they were then. I hope you'll forgive me missing out or under-emphasising any aspects that interest you.

2: 'PHASE ONE'[4]

The first quite obvious point to make about *Carnival of Monsters* is that the version we have has arisen out of necessity, through a series of compromises. It's not quite the story as first conceived, it's not quite the script as written and it's not quite the script as recorded, having been restructured during the post-recording editing process. It's an artefact of a **process**.

We're lucky with *Carnival of Monsters* to have quite a number of other surviving artefacts that help to illuminate that process. In the first instance, correspondence between the serial's script editor, Terrance Dicks, and the writer Robert Holmes is preserved at the BBC Written Archives Centre[5], including an early synopsis with appended notes that sheds some light on the evolution of the story[6]. The archive also holds camera scripts for all four episodes, detailing most of what was shot and making clear the intended story order as the programme went into studio. These scripts don't always retain details of scenes shot on location or reflect changes made to them during filming. As working documents used in the studio the scripts only really had to make sure the film sequences required were identifiable and played in for transfer to videotape,

---

[4] The Doctor, episode 4.

[5] Unless otherwise stated all the Written Archive material cited comes from the file T65/69/1 'Dr Who *Carnival of Monsters* 1971-1973'.

[6] Much of this, including a detailed early storyline, features in Richard Molesworth's excellent *Robert Holmes: A Life in Words* (2013), pp174-96. The copy in the BBC Written Archive Centre records also features several handwritten thoughts appended to Holmes' storyline by Terrance Dicks.

and one sequence in episode 3 is represented only by a handwritten note on the script covering the action in a single sentence: 'FILM DRASHIGS – DOCTOR/JO ESCAPE TO CAVE'. This stands in for three pages of the rehearsal script.

Rehearsal scripts for episodes 2, 3 and 4 existing in private hands reveal more clues to the serial's development, both preserving the initial script for the sequence missing from the camera scripts and making clear where the input of performers and production team reshaped Holmes' script[7]. In addition, we have a published script extract that seems to preserve a small section of episode 1's rehearsal script and a novelisation by the serial's script editor that appears to have been made with access to both sets of scripts.

The script extract, from the opening of episode 1 in Hulke's *Writing for Television in the 70s*, matches the camera script verbatim, bar the short sequence of stage directions relating to the revolutionary Functionary that give the proceeding chapter its title, 'A STREAM OF INCOMPREHENSIBLE BUT OBVIOUSLY REVOLUTIONARY GOBBLEDEYGOOK.' This stage direction covers the Functionary's address to its fellows below. In this printed extract, the novelisation and onscreen the Functionary goes 'BERSERK'[8], ascends the city wall, and attempts to make a speech before being shot by Kalik and falling. The camera script excludes any indication of him speaking, with stage directions stating the Functionary intends to jump from the wall (though how this might be relayed visually is left unclear). It also features an attempt by other Functionaries to restrain him with a net before Kalik shoots. It's possible Hulke chose to simplify

---

[7] My heartfelt thanks go to the kindly researcher who made these invaluable documents available to me.

[8] 'BERSERK' in camera script, 'BESERK?' in Hulke.

a series of complex stage directions and inserted a sly moment of humour in the process, but the version he presents is also reflected on screen. Stuntman Stuart Fell's Functionary does indeed gesticulate to a soundtrack of excitable grunting. It's possible the sequence with the net was a planned revision to the script to get additional value from hiring a stuntman for the Functionary's fall. If so it would seem that while it survived in stage directions, it was rejected well before studio. There's no prop requirement for a net detailed in the programme's production file and the capture is covered in the camera script by a single shot (a big close up on the revolutionary Functionary) which seems an odd choice given the sequence apparently planned. The combination of stunt work at height with action involving extras in masks and costumes that might impair visibility and mobility probably ruled the sequence out.

Terrance Dicks' novelisation of *Carnival of Monsters* is clearly made with access to Holmes' scripts, closely paraphrasing some stage directions, broadly retaining the original intended scene order (though Dicks chooses to open the narrative on the SS *Bernice* rather than Inter Minor) and incorporating material lost in the edit. However, it differs markedly from the camera scripts in descriptions of some events in episodes 1 and 3. Dicks' recounting of the previously discussed Functionary scene certainly tallies with Hulke's version of it, rather than the camera script: 'Vorg and Shirna could understand nothing of the Functionary's guttural speech, but judging from the growls of agreement the crowd was on his side.'[9]

---

[9] Dicks, Terrance, *Doctor Who and the Carnival of Monsters*, p14.

Leaving paperwork aside, we're also exceptionally fortunate to have producer and director Barry Letts' first edit of episode 2. This version famously retains the ultimately rejected 'Delaware'[10] reworking of the **Doctor Who** signature tune, but is also interesting for its only partially completed incidental score, and for the retention of scenes moved into episode 1 when the serial was restructured for timing reasons[11].

Another surprise survival from the production process is the recording of composer Dudley Simpson's incidental score for episode 1. Like the early edit of episode 2 this is a work in progress, presenting Simpson's sessions with conventional musicians before the additional of electronic effects by the BBC Radiophonic Workshop. *Carnival of Monsters* is an interesting transitional story for Simpson's music. It marks a return to him working with a group of musicians, after a period of primarily producing electronic music working closely with Brian Hodgson of the BBC Radiophonic Workshop. Simpson had already reintroduced conventional percussion in the story *Day of the Daleks* (1972), recorded in 1971,

---

[10] A reworked version of **Doctor Who**'s signature tune requested from the Radiophonic Workshop by Letts for the programme's 10th series, and executed by its original arranger Delia Derbyshire and colleagues Brian Hodgson and Paddy Kingsland. (See Chapter 3.)

[11] This early version of episode 2 was supplied in error to ABC TV for broadcast in Australia and was similarly released on the BBC's commercial VHS tape of the serial in the place of the transmission version. This had the unfortunate effect of adding scenes of the characters on Inter Minor repeating themselves to the scenes of the Tellurians repeating themselves in the Scope. Anyone unfortunate enough to stumble on this version of the story first is likely to have suspected something even more complicated going on temporally than was ultimately delivered.

but this is the first of his 1970s scores to be essentially performed on conventional instruments. It may be the adoption of more traditionally produced music occurred because Hodgson was leaving the BBC and his replacement providing Special Sound for **Doctor Who**, Dick Mills, was less musically minded. It almost certainly helped that a soundtrack using traditional instruments could be put together more easily. *Carnival of Monsters* sees Hodgson's final direct work on **Doctor Who**, though he ultimately returned to the BBC and the Radiophonic Workshop in 1977.

Several reels of model work filming for the serial were also retained, as well as a number of short filmed extracts of recording from the perspective of both the control room and studio floor[12]. (The model film extracts may well have been retained because Barry Letts was keen to reuse footage of the Drashigs, a piece of special effects work he was pleased with[13].) The studio behind-the-scenes sequences were shot for *Looking In*, a programme broadcast as part of BBC One's long-running Tuesday documentary strand on 7 November 1972, nearly 12 weeks before *Carnival of Monsters* aired. Presented in the *Radio Times* as part of a celebration of the

---

[12] Selections of mute model footage featuring the composition of the opening shuttle descent and the filmed Drashig puppet work are included on the BBC's two-disc special edition DVD release of *Carnival of Monsters*, alongside brief scenes from the studio floor and gallery filmed during the programme's second recording session.

[13] Visions of the Drashigs appear in two further **Doctor Who** stories produced by Barry Letts, *Frontier in Space* (1973) and *Planet of the Spiders* (1974). The latter of these is directed by Letts and reuses footage from *Carnival of Monsters*. It may have been that the reels of model work were preserved specifically to allow this kind of anticipated reuse direct from the film.

BBC's 50th anniversary (radio broadcasts had officially begun on 14 November 1922), *Looking In* examined BBC TV's output since its opening on 2 November 1936[14]. *Looking In* incorporates programme clips, commentary and discussion of TV and its role by members of the public, as well as a handful of specially shot interviews. It also features a number of establishing shots of BBC Television Centre and racked film and tape archives that have reappeared many times in documentaries since, and (as seems traditional in archive TV documentaries) makes considerable use of the BBC's 1936 film *Television Comes to London*. Two sets of contemporary behind–the–scenes footage are included – the **Nine O'Clock News** going out live and scenes from the *Carnival of Monsters* studio session devoted to recording the Inter Minor sequences.

The clips include shots of Leslie Dwyer and Michael Wisher in rehearsal, the TARDIS prop being positioned on set, glimpses of a Colour Separation Overlay (CSO) shot of a Drashig with a model of Kalik in its jaws being lined up, and Stuart Fell in partial Functionary costume preparing his stunt fall. Oddly, the shot of the model Kalik in the Drashig's mouth (which ultimately goes unused) is not readily apparent in the camera script. Because CSO shots would tie up two cameras, all these Drashigs in the city shots for episode 4 scene 18 were recorded together in sequence after the rest of the scene, but the planned shot list doesn't make clear when this might have been recorded. It seems likely from the background framing

---

[14] Confusingly, *Radio Times* used the 1936 date and referred to the film as a celebration of 30 years of TV. Pedantically, it would either have been 36 or just shy of 29 if BBC TV's wartime closedown were accounted for.

that it accompanied another similar shot establishing that the Drashigs have got loose, that appears earlier in the scene, but we have little detail to work with. Certainly Letts restructures much of the sequence in the edit, with Kalik's flight from the Drashig moved from what appears to be its intended position. This explains the oddly jarring moment where we seem to lose our established sense of space as we abruptly cut to him running. There's also no obvious candidate for a shot capturing the moment the episode 4 scripts cover with the stage direction 'IT EATS HIM', which the model Kalik shot seems to follow on from. Although a cursory glance might suggest this shot is the one in question, it is in the wrong part of the Inter Minor set to tie in with where Kalik meets his end. On his DVD commentary, Letts recalls the quality of the model as the issue with the shot, but it's just possible it was rejected not solely for deficiencies in the model work but also for continuity reasons.

The sequence also includes Barry Letts deciding on the fly to drop a reaction shot of Vorg in a scene in which Pletrac informs him of the quarantine arrangements for his departure (episode 4, scene 6).

3: 'THE TARDIS MAKES ITS AWESOME NOISE'[15]

The existence of Dudley Simpson's soundtrack recording for episode 1 appears to be the result of a happy accident[16]. Because Simpson worked closely with Brian Hodgson, tapes of the music he recorded in session at Lime Grove studios would then be taken to the Radiophonic Workshop on Delaware Road, Maida Vale, to have treatments and synthesiser overdubs applied. At this point most of Hodgson's work was being done on the EMS Synthi 100 synthesiser nicknamed 'the Delaware' because of the Workshop's location. Delia Derbyshire, the original arranger of the **Doctor Who** signature tune, was also working extensively in the room that held the EMS Synthi 100, and it appears Simpson's tape mistakenly ended up with Derbyshire's. The project Derbyshire had been working on was the so called 'Delaware version' of the **Doctor Who** theme tune, created by her and fellow composer Paddy Kingsland at Barry Letts' request. Hodgson and Derbyshire both left the BBC in 1973 (Hodgson immediately after working on *Carnival of Monsters*), and

---

[15] Stage direction, rehearsal script, episode 2, scene 26, p41. The TARDIS is making its 'awesome noise' as it expands because Holmes' rehearsal scripts associate the miniaturisation process with the TARDIS flight. Sadly, the connection is lost in the process of production: as broadcast, the noise made is a much less awesome ascending tone.

[16] An extract from the score appears on the 11-disc CD version of Silva Screen's **Doctor Who** 50th anniversary soundtrack collection. Simpson worked with five musicians on it, ordering an electric piano, Yamaha organ, bass marimba, 32 inch timpani, log drum, bell tree, sleigh bells, 2 cymbals on stands and bean pod for the session.

the tape was discovered when Mark Ayres and Dr David Butler of the Music and Drama department of Manchester University began cataloguing Derbyshire's archive in March 2007. By email in 2017, Brian Hodgson speculated that Derbyshire's final clear-up on leaving the BBC was not carefully done but 'just a wholesale grab of anything lying around in the areas in which she worked in case it was important'[17]. Sadly, tapes of Hodgson's special sound for the serial do not survive, a rare gap in the Radiophonic archive. The chief ambient backgrounds were tuned hums for the Scope interior and a looping city background for the Inter Minorian background which features a couple of electric vehicles moving. For the bleak marsh sequences Hodgson reused the mournful tuned-wind effect he devised for **Doctor Who**'s second story, *The Daleks* (1963-64)[18].

The great triumph of the soundtrack is his unearthly Drashig roars which combined treated versions of Hodgson's own voice, his corgi bitch, an Australian butcherbird and, as Barry Letts recalled it, a squeal of car brakes. Whether deliberately, to help blend the elements, or just as result of slowing down tapes, the roar also has a curious long reverb, suggestive of a large echoing space. Perhaps the one weakness of the Drashig sound effects is that this reverb remains constant whether the Drashigs are in open country, within the SS Bernice hold, or roaming the Inter Minorian city.

As we know from the surviving early video edit of *Carnival of Monsters* 2, the Delaware mix of the **Doctor Who** theme was

---

[17] Email to the author, 6 April 2017.
[18] The piece appears at different lengths on a number of soundtrack CDs, listed as both 'Skaro – Petrified Forest Atmosphere' and, rather more bathetically, 'Thal Wind'. The fullest version is on the 2017 soundtrack release *Doctor Who: The Daleks*.

initially applied to the serial. The original theme arrangement was reapplied to the completed episodes after the BBC Head of Serials expressed his distaste for the new version.

4: 'NIENTE DINARI'[19]

Carnival of Monsters is the shape it is as a piece of television because of the television culture and practice of the time, and the ambition of its producer and director to exploit that.

Barry Letts, as the man running **Doctor Who**, was acutely aware of the budgetary, logistical and technical limitations the show worked with, but as a director he was also aware of unrealised potential within the electronic studio.

The arrival of relatively straightforward non-physical tape editing meant Letts' period on **Doctor Who** was the first to really exploit out-of-sequence recording. Earlier eras of **Doctor Who** had been principally recorded 'as live' with a small number of 'fade to black' edit points across an episode. Out-of-sequence recording did occur on occasion, but was largely shunned because it was both time consuming and costly when working with physical tape. Videotape had to be physically cut and then re-spliced with extreme precision to prevent picture roll, and the join at the edit point produced in a glitch in the tape that meant it could not be subsequently reused on other shows (then routine because of tape costs). If a tape was edited, the cost of the tape would be charged to the production. Consequently tapes were rarely edited.

Rather than rehearsing for a week before going into studio for a camera rehearsal and then shooting an episode largely in story order, Letts instituted the practice of rehearsing for two weeks then following that with two days in studio. The days would be devoted to technical rehearsal followed by evening recordings,

---

[19] Vorg, episode 4.

with scenes typically grouped by location and then assembled in story order later during editing. In Letts' memoir *Who and Me*[20], he recalls set problems on his first **Doctor Who** production, *Doctor Who and the Silurians* (1970), when the story's cave sets were deemed too complex and extensive for what the BBC classed as a 'small drama'. Getting around the problem involved recording all the cave sequences in one session, so they needn't be repeatedly assembled and disassembled, and then editing them into the serial as required. Ultimately, even this didn't fully resolve the set problems, but this early crisis and its partial solution informed what became Letts' standard practice.

Using the studio space carefully allowed the production team to record material required for multiple episodes of a serial more efficiently, so in practice scenes from any number of episodes that shared a set could be recorded together.

A typical four-episode **Doctor Who** story would be rehearsed and recorded across a pair of two-day studio sessions; in the case of *Carnival of Monsters* these were on 19 and 20 June 1972, and 3 and 4 July 1972. If the scripts accommodated, many sets could now be built and struck for the first studio session without needing to be stored and recreated for the second. With fewer sets needed for each recording block, those that were built could potentially take up more floor space, benefit from a more concentrated construction period and be disassembled after use without fear of damage.

Letts' initial idea for what became *Carnival of Monsters* took this efficiency measure one step further by applying it to actors too.

---

[20] Letts, Barry, *Who and Me*, p82.

Letts wanted a four-episode show where the guest cast hired would only be needed for one of the two recording sessions. This neatly avoided having to pay to retain the actors for a full four weeks. The series regulars, Jon Pertwee and Katy Manning, would naturally appear across all four episodes, but would interact with two different sets of characters in two different locations, with the material from the two studio sessions interwoven.

The storyline Robert Holmes proposed based on these restrictions also appears to have been designed to be realised entirely within studio[21]. This would again be for financial reasons and would allow the serial's allocated film budget to be used elsewhere on the series.

Doctor Who regularly juggled its film allocation in this fashion. Extensive exterior action in one serial or episode was often made possible by realising others entirely in the studio; for example, *The Deadly Assassin* (1976)'s lengthy filmed Matrix sequences were achievable only because the surrounding episodes were entirely made in studio (as indeed were all eight episodes of the next two serials). The production block that included *Carnival of Monsters* had already featured one studio-realised story, *The Curse of Peladon* (1972), which featured brief clifftop and fight sequences

---

[21] As an experienced TV writer Holmes was adept at thinking within budgetary constraints. One fine example occurs in *Terror of the Autons* (1971) episode 2, where he transparently devises the character Tony to be played by an extra ('Tony don't talk much...') even though, in the final event, Barry Letts still chose to cast an actor in the role. Letts recalled the project as being planned solely for studio ('Destroy All Monsters!' (2007) DVD extra, *Carnival of Monsters* Special Edition DVD.)

shot on film at the BBC's Ealing studios but no location work. **Doctor Who** was by no means unique in this. The 1970s comedy series **The Goodies** (1970-80) often featured entirely studio-based and largely verbal episodes alongside more spectacular ones featuring lengthy filmed sequences of visual comedy. Even in the 1980s, more high-profile and better-budgeted series like **Boys from the Blackstuff** (1982) worked in a similar fashion, with one episode designed to be entirely studio-based, others designed to be made on outside broadcast (OB) video and the series' entire film allocation devoted to the episode *Yosser's Story*.

In the storyline, the SS *Bernice* is represented by a single section of deck, a saloon, a cabin and a passageway, interspersed with establishing shots of the sea and the sun setting, presumably to be sourced from stock. The TARDIS arrives on the deck in daylight and is subsequently removed by Vorg's giant hand by night, a combination of costly night filming and effects work which Holmes is unlikely to have proposed if he'd expected the material to be shot on location. Holmes is also at pains to indicate he sees the swampy location for the Drashigs as monochrome and obscured by mists, presumably so it can be represented in the studio without extensive design work. This thinking probably accounts for the Drashigs being animals that hunt by smell rather than sight – they have been created for a world where there's very little to see[22].

It's just possible Holmes may also have had something a little

---

[22] The storyline is presented in its entirety in Molesworth, *Robert Holmes*, pp181-96. Correspondence from Terrance Dicks to Holmes indicates it was already being discussed by 2 July 1971, though it was not officially submitted to the BBC until 1 September. Again, this was not uncommon in the television practices of the time.

playful in mind with the monochrome world of the Drashigs. The final script features a little jokey comparison of viewing the Scope to watching TV, with Shirna's line 'Who's going to pay good credit bars to see a blob in a snowstorm?'[23], and it could well be that Holmes also hoped to echo the regular complaint of contemporary viewers paying extra for colour TV licences, that they were still having to watch shows and films made in black-and-white.

The decision to go out on location had clearly been taken by the time Holmes came to write the actual episodes in November 1971. The scripts take greater advantage of varied deck settings than the storyline, and the additional small part of the SS *Bernice*'s captain has been devised so he appears only on location (again to avoid paying to retain the actor). Holmes has also moved the TARDIS' arrival scene into the ship's hold, where its removal by CSO is somewhat easier to accommodate.

The challenges of constructing a convincing ship's deck and swamp world in studio were probably factors in this decision to abandon an entirely studio-based production. It's also possible Barry Letts' decision to direct as well as produce was a factor[24]. He certainly

---

[23] Episode 2. The line echoes contemporary viewer complaints about poor TV reception (indeed, a member of the public describes a poor picture as a 'snowstorm' in the Vox Pop commentary that accompanies *Looking In*).

[24] Barry Letts had moved from a career in directing to produce **Doctor Who**, but, while relishing the challenges of the new role, retained a passion for direction. Letts accepted the Producer role with the proviso that he could continue directing (which he considered wise for career reasons), and his BBC contract specifically allowed him to direct a **Doctor Who** serial a year. Practically, these directorial roles would end up at either the start

knew that the planned production dates in the summer of 1972 would allow for longer filming days.

The decision to use filmed locations certainly enhances the serial visually, producing some arresting images and giving additional punch to the wonderful first surprise cliffhanger, but it probably also informs the disappointment some commentators have expressed with regard to the serial.

---

or end of production blocks, where Letts' commitment to a single serial as a director would be less likely to impact on his oversight of other serials' production. It's possible he selected this serial to work on to retain close hands-on control of the split cast production experiment.

5: 'IT WASN'T THE REAL OUTSIDE, WAS IT?'[25]

Hardly anyone reading this can now be unaware that *Carnival of Monsters* is set partially within an artificial miniature world on an alien planet. This condition of having had the brilliant narrative twist spoiled for you is one you probably share with most viewers of the serial since 1981[26], almost of all whom will have come to the show having read a published synopsis or the back-cover blurb of a novelisation or videocassette that gives it away[27]. Some of you may even have been unfortunate enough to have read the original episode 1 listing in the *Radio Times* listing magazine in 1972:

---

[25] Jo, episode 3.

[26] In 1981 *Carnival of Monsters* was repeated on BBC 2 opposite BBC One's early evening news, and drew audiences of 4.5 to 6 million who presumably wanted nothing political and nothing serious. Those audiences were probably the last to come to the serial in any number without at least some idea of what was to come.

[27] To their credit the blurbs on the back of both UK DVD releases of *Carnival of Monsters* managed to avoid revealing the big end-of-episode surprise when the serial's two narrative strands first explicitly combine. As scripted, the episode 1 ending is slightly less out of the blue. A cut sequence in what was to have been scene 6 reveals Inter Minor to be in the Acteon system, suggesting the Doctor is not as far wrong about their location as Jo believes. Losing this advance pointer for more astute viewers probably makes the cliffhanger even more effective.

'The TARDIS lands on a cargo-ship in the Indian Ocean, in the year 1926. Or does it? Fellow passengers act strangely – a monster appears from the deep – and alien giants look on dispassionately.'[28]

It's a revelation that I believe is made all the stronger because of the way we tend to read film and studio in 20th-century TV. Most viewers have an ear and eye for it. They detect the differences in the way film and videotape handle colour and movement. They notice the greater range of angles available to a tripod-mounted film camera than to a pedestal-mounted EMI 2001 video camera. They can hear, even without knowing it, the sound of a studio space pretending to be smaller or larger than it really is. They pick up on the flatter, general lighting of a space designed for multiple studio cameras to move through, as opposed to the directional or natural light of real locations filmed by a single camera. We're primed to see what happens in a real world as 'film' and what occurs in a constructed space as 'videotape'. Thus, when *Carnival of Monsters* opens on a very artificial-looking studio-based planet with model shots, yellow-fringed CSO and studio rostra purporting to be a real outdoor space, it asks viewers to make an imaginative leap and suspend their disbelief if they're going to go along with the reality of the environment.

Even the framing of shots on Inter Minor reads theatrically rather than filmically. The discussions between the Inter Minorian[29]

---

[28] 'Dr Who: Carnival of Monsters – Episode 1', BBC Genome Project. Most contemporary viewers are likely to have seen the serial without reading this leading entry.
[29] I follow the scripts in using 'Minorian'. The oft-adopted alternative 'Minoran' originates in Dicks' novelisation.

tribunal are often composed as a classic TV 'deep three shot' in which a background figure faces fully forward while talking to two foreground figures[30]. The action is being served up to us through the screen in a modified television form of the proscenium arch, theatre's imaginary fourth wall. It's a shot popular in studio drama that pops up regularly in soap opera simply because it's easily achievable (all the sets really do have imaginary 'fourth walls' to allow the cameras access) and it allows us to follow the reactions of actors in real time. Film, usually constructed piecemeal with a single camera on TV, generally resists this kind of shot, cutting away to follow individual reactions, with the filmmakers secure in the knowledge they're shooting in a location that has exactly the number of walls you might expect[31].

Naturalism is also regularly cheated on the surface of Inter Minor by characters' selective deafness as others conspire yards from each other, unheard. The planet seems to have adopted the long-established TV studio grammar that deems that a character cannot

---

[30] These are usually shot in slightly 'cheated' profiles allowing the viewer to see most of the foreground actors' faces, but in *Carnival of Monsters* they're usually in true profile, quite an alienating device that emphasises their curious regulated formality.

[31] **Doctor Who** had experimented with multi-camera location filming under Letts, in *The Dæmons* (1971), a serial co-written by Letts pseudonymously and directed by Christopher Barry. The number of scenes written for location meant the greater speed of multi-camera film work offset the expense of additional film stock to some extent. In later years **Doctor Who** would slowly move away from location filming to work with video on location: *Robot* (1974-75), *The Sontaran Experiment* (1975), *The Seeds of Doom* (1976) and *The Stones of Blood* (1978) all make use of OB video, before location video becomes the series' norm in the late 1980s.

hear anything that occurs if they are even an inch offscreen or are out of focus in the background.

Attention is drawn to this oddity of TV style, as seen in the work of director Mervyn Pinfield, on the DVD commentaries for *The Sensorites* and *Planet of Giants* (both 1964). It probably arises from enforced working in limited studio space in TV's earliest days, but continued to linger as a useful convention viewers would be prepared to accept for some time after. The depiction of 'overhearing' in TV work that follows this convention generally requires either a cutaway to pointed 'listening' acting, or a deep background figure in a three shot coming suddenly into sharp focus.

It's quite possible this artificial device arose out of a feature of the original storyline that survives vestigially in the camera script. When we first meet Vorg and Shirna in Holmes' storyline, he has them and the Scope (at this stage known as the Strobe[32], a name that survives in stage directions for episode 2 and 3[33]) in what's described as a Vol-Dome, a futuristic structure that's presumably self-erected on the planet they're visiting[34]. The storyline later

---

[32] It's also called the Glo-Sphere in Holmes' notes, a reference to its viewing screen which Holmes presumably intended to be a sphere showing 3D images. The practicalities of TV production reduce this to a more manageable sphere with a circular screen cut in that shows images that have been distorted with a fisheye lens effect.

[33] 'THE STROBE' is used in stage directions for episode 1, scene 6, episode 2, scene 2, and episode 3, scene 15. The setting for episode 2, Scene 4, in which we see the Ogron and Cyberman within their Scope environments, is described in scene headings as 'INT. STROBE LIMBO.'

[34] In Holmes' storyline the Vol-Dome is endearingly described as

refs to Shirna looking out on massing potential customers and the planet's bureaucrats through a peephole, and the camera script for Episode 1 refers to a crowd massing by a door to the Scope's location.

Vol-Dome, despite never being a term used on screen, is a name used inconsistently on production documents as a shorthand for the Inter Minor scenes usually described in the script as 'EXT. CITY. DAY.', but two scenes tellingly heading 'INT. VOL-DOME. MURK.' suggest Holmes still pictures the Vol-Dome as a distinct enclosed location on the planet.

The first of the scenes (episode 2, scene 16) is a short sequence in which Vorg adjusts the aggrometer. The camera script chooses to frame the sequence with close-ups of Vorg and a control on the Scope, treating 'INT. VOL-DOME. MURK' as an ordinary city exterior shot. It's just possible, if a bit of an imaginative leap, to consider the script heading 'INT. VOL-DOME. MURK'. may be indicating Holmes wanted this shot framed as though observed from within the Scope. If so it's an artistic flourish he suggests nowhere else. The setting recurs in episode 3, scene 15, which has Shirna and Vorg discussing the plight of the specimens in the Scope. Shirna initially looks into the Scope through an inspection plate which might again invite the interpretation of the scene as a Scope POV shot if it weren't for the stage direction shortly after, 'SHIRNA SITS

'the equivalent of a fairground tent but like scientific' (Molesworth, *Robert Holmes* p184). At this stage the Inter Minorians are called Lurmans; the planet is later renamed Odron in Holmes notes. Both the storyline and Holmes' notes state the Vol-Dome is here because the planet is hosting a showmen's convention, a notion ultimately dropped from the story.

DOWN AGAINST THE STROBE', which reinforces the suspicion that Holmes still had details of his initial storyline in his mind at the time of writing. It's possible these small anomalies point to these scenes being survivors from an earlier draft. The Vol-Dome setting as a separate interior may well have gone missing following Dicks' notes on Holmes storyline. Dicks makes clear that the alien world Holmes has originally held back until episode 2 should appear earlier and should be a 'stunning CSO alien set'. Given that note, one can easily imagine Holmes deciding to replace the murky Vol-Dome interior with alfresco Scope demonstrations in the city set we see on screen.

Once we head out to the filmed 'exterior' of the SS *Bernice* we're working with a different type of TV grammar. Following the convention viewers have come to accept and expect, the ship's interior rooms are shot on videotape (and obey similar rules to the surface of Inter Minor), but its exterior is a filmed location, exploiting wide shots and multiple angles and more likely to cover conversations in cutaway single shots[35]. In fact one could almost be forgiven for feeling that, as well as switching between locations, the two initially unlinked narratives come from two entirely different shows working to different sets of rules as they cut jarringly from scenes with the ruddy-faced Major Daly to grey-faced Inter Minorians[36].

Furthermore, the SS *Bernice* scenes are set in what seems to be a

---

[35] The dynamically-angled shots on the deck of the SS *Bernice* also serve the very practical purpose of concealing the banks of the River Medway that would reveal the filming location to be somewhat closer to home than the Indian Ocean.

[36] 'How strange the change from Major to Minor...'

very real, lived-in space, with detailed, recognisable naturalistic sets and costumes that project historical accuracy.

The scenes on Inter Minor follow different design rules: as Piers D Britton and Simon J Barker put it, they 'would not have looked out of place on a light entertainment show'[37]. Roger Liminton's sets work with deliberately simplified shapes and a reduced colour palette, and James Acheson's costumes follow that for the Inter Minorians and fight it aggressively with the busy and colourful outfits of Vorg and Shirna. Liminton explains a preference for stylised settings in a brief interview in the 1973 *Radio Times Doctor Who Special*:

> '**Doctor Who** appeals so much because it allows me to use my analytical approach to design. I suppose I'm slightly puritanical in my approach anyway, but I've never leaned towards period drama. [...] I like a clean, crisp look. I'm a tidy little fellow.'

Liminton creates a stripped-back world of vertical lines and curves, which Acheson follows in his Inter Minorian costumes. In creating costumes for Vorg and Shirna, Acheson seems to have been responding to the extreme utilitarianism of Inter Minor, creating outfits full of what Inter Minorians and a number of fan commentators might consider pointless and silly ornamentation[38].

---

[37] Britton, Piers D, and Simon J Barker, *Reading Between Designs: Visual Imagery and the Generation of Meaning in The Avengers, The Prisoner, and Doctor Who*, p175.

[38] Liminton's full piece was available until recently on the *Radio Times* website as a jpeg image. Unfortunately the link to it from http://www.radiotimes.com/news/2010-01-20/carnival-of-

The overall effect is actually quite close to broadly contemporary TV spoofs of science fiction, where space ladies in silver boots stride through CSO spaces in the company of comically made-up aliens[39].

When contemporary viewers finally discovered the film world was artificial, and by implication existed within the stagey videotaped alien planet, their unconscious expectations were likely to have been well and truly overturned. The effect may have been arrived at by a gradual process of script development, and may of course have been unintentional, but it's still a striking one – everything that looked familiar and read as real in episode 1 is a fake.

Holmes seems to play a similar trick with the texture of film and video in a later **Doctor Who** story, *The Deadly Assassin*, in which Gallifrey, the home planet of the Time Lords, is entirely realised on videotape until the Doctor ends the hallucinatory computer reality of the Matrix, and is suddenly plunged into a whole new world of location film. The structure of episode 1 may also have influenced a further **Doctor Who** story. Whether by accident, design or sheer coincidence, the opening episode of *Enlightenment* (1983) echoes *Carnival of Monsters* with the TARDIS' arrival in the hold of a sailing-ship where all is not quite as it should be, culminating in an impossible reveal that the ship is actually out in space.

It's conjecture on my part but I think it is the very naturalistic quality of the SS *Bernice* locations, and the recognisable period

---

monsters/ is broken at the time of going to press.

[39] The specific examples I have in mind are Howard Schuman's 1976 Granada TV play *Amazing Stories* and Nigel Kneale's 1980 LWT series **Kinvig**.

costumes and interior sets that go along with it, that heighten some viewers' distaste for the electronic studio-mounted scenes on Inter Minor which feature heightened design and performances. The deliberate shift in textures which I find adds considerable interest, clearly strikes some as jarring and uneven[40].

Was *Carnival of Monsters* a success? Naturally, it depends on your point of view. It gained impressive audiences on both its BBC TV transmissions, and it's remembered positively by many **Doctor Who** fans to date, arguably setting the tone for a new kind of **Doctor Who** story – ridiculous and witty but played straight, written to contain much that went over the head of a child viewer but embracing their need for wonder, action and fear. Holmes' next script for the series, *The Time Warrior* (1973-74), has a similar tone, and a comparable style re-emerges in the late 70s and 80s under script editors Anthony Read, Douglas Adams and Andrew Cartmel.

It was certainly not a trouble-free production, and failed to save money as initially hoped. Location filming costs were inflated by an unexpected rearrangement of filming dates costing the production £109, and a dispute over lost life jackets issued for the marsh filming resulted in an additional bill of £62.40 also being charged to the production[41]. The second and final days in studio also overran

---

[40] One additional factor is of course less-than-perfect early visual effects work. The initial CSO is poor, the Functionary masks are unconvincing and some elements of the set do not seem wholly robust. For a large number of viewers this will be immediately alienating.

[41] Bignell, Richard, *Doctor Who on Location* (2001), p97. The circumstances of the life jackets' loss were disputed, and it's unclear today how the situation was resolved and indeed whether the production paid the additional bill.

expensively by 15 and 80 minutes respectively, which Letts put down to the complexity of various CSO effects and lengthy recording breaks in the first instance, and the time consumed lining up Drashig puppet shots and transferring multiple film sequences to tape for all four episodes in the second instance[42].

As a production it has a number of rough edges, quite literally in episode 4 where we see snapped polystyrene on the sets and a metal cylinder lid which is patently painted cardboard, and the join of the Officials' bald caps becomes ever more obvious[43].

However the performances are strong, the writing generally tight and some of the thrills and jokes are wonderful. Quite fittingly, it's a game of two halves.

---

[42] Jon Pertwee used to recount a story of how the overnight bag of a Drashig puppeteer was mistaken for an IRA bomb, leading to an evacuation of the studios, though sad to say this seems to be another tale that grew in the telling. It's an incident no one else involved seem to have recalled, and one suspects that if it had occurred Barry Letts would have cited the disruption it would have caused as a factor behind one of his studio over-runs. He did not.

[43] So much so that for the repeat run in 1981, Barry Letts requested an edit to the final scene of episode 4 to remove the most obvious shots of Pletrac's bald cap wrinkling as it began to come unstuck from Peter Halliday's head. It's an odd decision for a couple of reasons. It's an edit to the very end of the programme when viewers likely to be put off by such visual deficiencies must surely have already changed channel or switched off in disgust. Naturally, it in no way makes the scenes on Inter Minor look more realistic – the obviously painted cardboard cylinder lid continues to be seen in unforgiving and lingering close ups throughout the edited scene. Finally, it somewhat weakens the story's ending, failing to make clear that Vorg is managing to win money off Pletrac with a trick as simple as 'Find the Lady'.

Barry Letts considered it a partial success:

> 'Like all things one's done in the past, I was a bit disappointed in the way some of [it] worked out, but it was nothing to do with the script, it was to do with odd things like make-up, and so on, that weren't quite as they should have been, but that's life!'[44]

Technically, there are some awkward moments in the editing; the perfunctory and confused attack of the Drashigs in episode 4 is a disappointing climax, and the combination of two scenes by the Scope in episode 1 feels particularly clumsy, as Shirna's position in the scene suddenly shifts between shots.

The reason this edit was required was a radical restructuring of the narrative in post-production.

Once edits of the episodes had been assembled from the two recording sessions it was clear two of them, episodes 2 and 4, were running seriously over their allotted time slots. Although small sections of episodes 2 and 4 could be trimmed, the remaining scenes contained vital plot information that couldn't be cut. Consequently, sections of episodes 1 and 3 that could be removed with minimal impact were removed and portions of episode 2 and 4 moved forward to help balance the running times. The construction of the scripts with events on Inter Minor and within the Scope only directly connecting at certain points made it easier to do this than would often be the case. On the other hand, it's quite likely this reworking was only required because the scripts had been written that way. For all it saved paying to retain artists,

---

[44] Molesworth, *Robert Holmes*, p179.

the innovation of piecemeal rehearsal with only partial casts and scripts must have made accurately judging the final running times of individual episodes much harder than normal.

Carnival of Monsters is one of the first **Doctor Who** serials we're aware of being radically restructured in the edit[45]. The only previous example of this level of work being done to a story post-recording is the edit of the original episodes 3 and 4 of *Planet of Giants* in 1964, which were felt to lack drive and were combined to make a more dynamic episode 3[46].

Rather than present all the edits and changes of order in a list here, I'll address major changes where they become relevant in the next section, which looks at how the narrative developed in broader terms. Readers interested in such a list will find it in the Appendix.

---

[45] In Barry Letts' final series as producer of **Doctor Who**, two serials — *Death to the Daleks* (1974) and *Planet of the Spiders* — both underwent edits for timing reasons in a similar fashion to *Carnival of Monsters*, both having a cliffhanger reconstructed.

[46] As mentioned in an earlier footnote, this edit was carried out on film.

6: 'WHY DOES IT KEEP CHANGING SIZE?'[47]

One thing we learn from comparing Holmes' storylines, the surviving scripts and the final edit of *Carnival of Monsters* is that the plot was in flux throughout production. Character, planet and location names fluctuate and their meanings drift through its iterations, and motivations, actions and back story all shift even when leading to the same outcome. The Scope is a Glo-Sphere or Strobe within a Vol-Dome right through to production, even though we viewers never learn what a Vol-Dome is and the production team seem unsure. It isn't even revealed to be a Miniscope until the camera script. The Vol-Dome drifts from being unambiguously Vorg's space to representing the Inter-Minorian city on both scripts and production documents. Echoes of earlier abandoned ideas survive throughout the finished programme, notably the Scope circuits, which the Doctor compares to a wristwatch in episode 2, scene 18. This is a ghost from Holmes' initial storyline which sees the Doctor and Jo negotiate hazardous cogs as they move around the machine. The same thinking informs Holmes' writing of the space in the rehearsal script. It is cramped, oily and features hanging chains – a mechanical space rather than the electronic one ultimately designed by Roger Liminton.

Perhaps the most surprising difference in these circuit scenes is that this one originally ended in a cut sequence when the Doctor recognises some of the components around him.

---

[47] Orum, episode 2.

DOCTOR WHO:[48]

...Well, we can try following these feedlines... Probably run for miles, though.

JO:

Doctor, you said 'one of these' – does that mean you know what this is?

DOCTOR WHO:

Well, this part looks as though it's from one of the early transveyors.. [sic]

JO:

What's a transveyor?

DOCTOR WHO:

The Omegans used them in the old days for transporting convicts to the outer planets. My Tardis [sic] is a more sophisticated example of the principle[49].

This piece of backstory is ultimately abandoned but traces of it continue to inform the story as broadcast. The rehearsal scripts go on to use the similarity of TARDIS and Omegan transveyor technology to justify the TARDIS being caught in the Scope's field, and the battery commander Vorg reminisces about in episode 4 is an Omegan rather than a Crustacioid[50]. The TARDIS having an

---

[48] Although **Black Archive** house style would normally render this as just 'DOCTOR', what follows is a verbatim quote from Holmes' rehearsal script.

[49] Unpublished rehearsal script, episode 2, scene 3.

[50] The camera script spelling. Dicks' novelisation goes for the more

43

Omega circuit from rehearsal script through to transmission was probably also intended to link to the Omegans and explain the compatibility of TARDIS technology and the Scope in episode 4 (a convenience that several fan commentators have criticised).

Several filmed inserts are radically reworked from the script, most notably the sequences in the Drashig swamp. Initially, after Jo had become exhausted from running, Holmes had the Doctor fire a Very pistol (a flare gun picked up on the SS *Bernice* that the Doctor has tucked in his belt) into a Drashig's mouth. This becomes the Doctor igniting marsh gas with his sonic screwdriver after Jo has got stuck in mud on location. The changes may have arisen for practical reasons – Jo's reworked jeopardy may just make better use of the location and the Doctor shooting the Drashig might have proven a challenge to realise on screen, but the televised versions also show the characters in a different light, making Jo seem less feeble and avoiding the Doctor carrying a gun for half an episode, which might have proved cumbersome and of concern to some viewers.

In all likelihood, the decision to remove the gun was made by either Barry Letts or Jon Pertwee to reduce the Doctor's perceived violence. The Doctor shooting the Drashig appears in the storyline Holmes presented to Dicks, and was accepted without quibble. In order to justify the igniting gas, a mute location sequence in the episode 2 rehearsal script has lines added that prefigure the presence of marsh gas. Although Holmes had not written igniting gas or the sinking in mud in these scenes, they do flow logically from his earlier versions – his descriptions of the swamp location from the storyline on describe the location as muddy, with

---

sensible 'Crustacoid.'

steaming geysers and sulphurous mists. Like the 'wristwatch' Scope interior, an echo of the lost first draft survives on transmission in the following scene (episode 3, scene 4) when Jo and the Doctor re-enter the circuits of the Scope, and the exhaustion that endangered her in earlier drafts returns[51].

The latter part of this scene is another that is heavily revised. In the rehearsal script the Doctor identifies their location as 'a series of self-perpetuating miniaturised environments', failing to name it as a Miniscope, and adding 'I wonder how they regulate at [sic] all.' The analogue of their location with ant colonies and peepshows is then made as televised, and there the scene ends. The corresponding page of the camera script is headed 'Rewrite to Ep. 3 PPP', and overwrites this sequence before adding dialogue. The listing of the main character's name on stage directions changes at this point from Holmes' habitual 'DOCTOR WHO' to 'DR. WHO', strongly indicating the extension to the scene that follows is the work of Terrance Dicks. This rewrite cuts the Doctor's musing on how the environments are regulated and names the Scope a Miniscope, before going on to emphasise the cruelty of captivity in one and raise notions of moral relativity. It then give Pertwee an excuse to do a carnival barker voice, offers the backstory of the Doctor having been involved in the banning of Miniscopes and suggests the TARDIS materialised in this one's compression field. It's an expansion of just over two pages that deftly clarifies the situation and provides the Doctor with moral and legal justifications for his involvement in it, beyond just trying to reclaim

---

[51] Her trousers have also miraculously cleaned up, making this Jo seem much more plausibly one exhausted from running than one who'd got stuck in a swamp.

his ship.

The next extended rewrite is perhaps less elegant and is chiefly designed to bring an episode running short up to time. In the rehearsal script for episode 3, scene 14, after looking down the deep shaft (rather than dropping a penny down it as televised) the Doctor realises they need a rope to get down it. Jo immediately remembers seeing some on the SS *Bernice* and the Doctor calls her a genius for this, a suggestion she deflects. Dicks' rewrite extends the scene by two pages, by having the Doctor and Jo expound on their problems and the Doctor explaining lateral thinking to Jo. Slightly misunderstanding it, she stumbles on the idea of returning to the ship and calls the Doctor brilliant for giving her the idea. Now he becomes the one deflecting praise. The revised version slightly unfortunately takes away some of Jo's agency and the Doctor's genuine admiration for her, while making her seem a little slow and literal-minded[52].

Another rewritten series of filmed sequences occurs later in episode 3, with the scenes covering the Drashig breaking out and the SS *Bernice* crew reacting. These appear to have been reworked for a number of reasons – to better use the geography of the location, exploit the availability of extras and to offer a little more dialogue and screen time to the actor playing the ship's captain,

---

[52] It may be worth noting that Dicks' writing of Jo in the *Carnival* novelisation generally paints her as rather less resourceful than she appears on screen. It might be that Holmes, who wrote the story introducing Jo, considers her to have more about her than Dicks, the series' regular script editor. Alex Wilcock comments insightfully on this depiction of Jo in '*Doctor Who and the Carnival of Monsters*'.

who appears only in these filmed scenes. (The actor in question is Anthony Staines, a favourite of Barry Letts', not least because he was Letts' nephew.)

The final major change to episode 3 is the removal in post-production of its planned and recorded cliffhanger ending and its episode 4 resolution. This allowed material from episode 4 which would have otherwise have overrun badly to be moved back into episode 3. A new cliffhanger was then constructed from the Doctor's staggering out of the Scope onto Inter Minor, and small trims were made to Jo's scenes on the SS *Bernice* in this episode.

It's likely one of the reasons episode 4 overran was a major revision to the rehearsal script. Surprisingly, the whole two-and-a-half-page sequence in which the Doctor establishes where he is, asserts his authority, bamboozles the Inter Minorian tribunal with intergalactic legal argument and seeks permission to rescue Jo from the Scope is an addition in the camera script[53]. Once again the script listing 'DR. WHO' instead of 'DOCTOR WHO' indicates this is Terrance Dicks' work, and once again it is a sequence that crucially clarifies several elements of the story. No version of this conversation whatsoever exists in Holmes' rehearsal script.

An equally striking change follows immediately after it. In the rehearsal script, Vorg's attempt to talk to the Doctor is quite different to that transmitted. Having decided the Doctor is a Tellurian showman, Vorg attempts to speak to the Doctor, but not in Palare as he does on screen:

---

[53] Camera script, episode 4, scene 3.

VORG:

You watch this. I'll talk to him in his own language.

(VORG SIDLES UP TO DOCTOR WHO)

VORG:

Hi-de-hi[54].

DOCTOR WHO:

I beg your pardon?

(VORG WINKS AND GRINS)

VORG:

Booby dooby boo.

DOCTOR WHO:

Eh?

VORG:

Swing-a-ding ding?

DOCTOR WHO:

I'm afraid I don't speak any of those languages, If you could just –

VORG CLAPS HIM ON THE SHOULDER)

---

[54] If this scene had been shot this would have been on the clip shows. Readers outside the UK may not be aware that Leslie Dwyer is best known in the UK for a regular role in the 1980s BBC sitcom, **Hi-de-Hi!** (1980-88).

VORG:

Aw come on fella! Why so uptight. [sic] You're a showman like me, ain't ya?[55]

The rehearsal room adaptation ultimately recorded loses a certain absurdity, but is, to my tastes, a pleasing refinement that manages to be both comic and logical. It is also a moment the cast recall Dwyer and Pertwee devised between them[56].

One final small change to episode 4 is worthy of note, for revealing another of our draft ghosts. As originally scripted, the Doctor's lash-up is damaged not after Pletrac shoots at the escaping Doctor but afterwards, when a petulant swipe at it with his gun short-circuits it[57]. Vorg and Shirna's discussion of the device's poor electrical insulation and his advice not to touch the bare metal, which survive to transmission, are intended to foreshadow this moment as much as set up the joke where Shirna touches a live terminal.

---

[55] Camera script, episode 4, scene 3.
[56] As recalled by Cheryl Hall (episode 4 audio commentary, special edition DVD release).
[57] Unpublished rehearsal script, episode 4, scene 10.

7: 'IT IS AN ALIEN ARTEFACT. WHERE DID IT COME FROM?'[58]

In terms of concrete inspirations for Holmes' storyline, it's hard not to speculate he was influenced by an episode of the BBC science fiction anthology series **Out of the Unknown** that aired during a period when he was likely to have been playing close attention to TV science fiction. In the mid-1960s, Holmes was a writer just beginning to work in this genre, having scripted *Invasion* (1966), a low-budget British science fiction movie (now mainly watched by people who want to compare it to his **Doctor Who** serial *Spearhead from Space* (1970)), and two episodes of **Undermind** (1965), an ABC TV serial devised by his friend Robert Banks Stewart. Holmes clearly saw potential for more work in the genre, pitching his own science fiction serial to the BBC around this date. His initial approach is missing, but 1965 correspondence survives between Holmes and **Doctor Who**'s script editor, Donald Tosh, relating to an attempt to repurpose the idea for the series. Although nothing came of this at the time, the idea eventually resurfaced as Holmes' first **Doctor Who** serial, *The Krotons*. A quotation from an unidentified fanzine interview in Hearn, 'Holmes on Holmes', has Holmes describe himself as 'a bit of a science fiction buff' during the early days of **Doctor Who**, saying he 'watched it occasionally' but 'always found it something of a disappointment.'[59]

The **Out of the Unknown** episode *Tunnel Under the World,* adapted by David Campton from Frederik Pohl's story 'The Tunnel Under the

---

[58] Pletrac , episode 2.
[59] Hearn, 'Holmes on Holmes', p36.

World' (1954)[60], was transmitted on BBC 1 December 1966. The play deals with a man named Guy Birkett (played by Ronald Hines) repeatedly living the same day (in this case 15 June), having his behaviour nudged by unseen controllers. Plagued by a sense of déjà vu and troubled by curious awry details in his surroundings (including an out-of-place metal wall behind fake brickwork), he ultimately discovers the titular tunnel under his world. He makes his way through a corridor in which an incongruous human-sized spanner leans against the wall and discovers the world outside. His whole town is a table-top model watched over by giant humans. Birkett discovers he's a mechanical simulacrum of a dead human recreated in a model environment which tests the power of media propaganda and using advertising as a hidden persuader. When Birkett attempts to end his artificial existence by jumping from the table-top model, a giant hand descends and pushes him back into his simulated environment. Soon afterwards, Birkett awakes to another 15 June[61].

---

[60] *Galaxy Science Fiction* volume 9 #4, cover date January, 1955, though clearly published in 1954 given the Christmas gift subscription offer within.

[61] Rather pleasingly, the play opens with the camera moving in on the town from above in what's obviously a model shot, if quite a good one. When viewers finally learn it was just a good model within the fiction as well as in reality, they've a nice opportunity to dis-suspend any disbelief they may have been suspending. It's an enjoyable lurch of confounded expectations, similar to the effect I'd argue the counter-intuitive mix of film and video has in *Carnival of Monsters*. Of course, if you've read all this before seeing *Tunnel Under the World* I've probably spoiled the moment for you as comprehensively as the old VHS back cover spoiled *Carnival of Monsters*.

Despite the differences in underlying cause, the similarities between the drama and Holmes' tale are suggestive – we have miniature humans with looped behaviour in a faked reality, and several striking shared moments – the unexpected metal panelling, the tunnel with a huge repair tool inside and the hand that reaches down to the model world. Of course, Holmes may not have seen the programme, but it seems quite plausible he could have, and memories of it, either conscious or otherwise, could have easily helped him reach a solution to the structural problem of a story in which characters needed to share linked but ultimately separate worlds.

Holmes may have been familiar with the original story, which had been reprinted on several occasions, most prominently in the UK in Brian Aldiss' 1963 anthology *More Penguin Science Fiction*. The prose story is broadly similar to its TV adaptation, but also features the hull of a boat in the lead character's cellar which he remembers having built himself but now discovers is a crudely finished fake[62]. The passage could feasibly start a chain of thought that leads to the creation of the much larger fake craft, the SS *Bernice*[63].

---

[62] The story does not, however, feature the TV version's discarded giant tool.

[63] We know from friends of Holmes that he (like Major Daly) enjoyed Indian food, and Molesworth's *Robert Holmes* informs us he kept souvenirs he'd 'acquired' during his time in the East, including what were described as a 'bulky' statue of a 'minor Chinese deity' and two Samurai swords. It's hard for a **Doctor Who** fan not to be reminded of Professor Litefoot in Holmes' *The Talons of Weng-Chiang* (1977) and his acquisitions from China, but exploring the likely nature of Holmes' service further raises questions about the 'acquisition' process.

Additional inspirations may have arisen during Holmes' time in the army during the Second World War. Holmes served with the Black Watch, Third Battalion Royal Regiment of Scotland, illegally signing up around 1942 when he was only 16. Posted in Burma and India, he developed an abiding interest in Eastern cultures that was reflected in both his life and work.

The attitude and language of British colonials Holmes would have come across in India would seem an obvious source for the passengers and crew of the SS *Bernice*. As a writer who seems to have delighted in period slang, Holmes is likely to have found the outdated vocabulary and attitudes both entertaining to work with and a gift for a group of characters set in their behaviour and out of their time.[64]

However, I suspect Holmes' time in India and Burma had another, more specific impact on the story[65]. Given those locations, it's likely

---

[64] It's sometimes been implied (not least by Holmes in recollection) that the Raj setting of *Carnival of Monsters* may have been influenced by his work on the BBC TV series **The Regiment** (1972-73). In fact Holmes didn't make his initial approach to that series' producer, Anthony Coburn, until May 1972, long after he'd delivered his scripts for *Carnival of Monsters* (Molesworth, *Robert Holmes* p171), presenting him with a 1968 script in a similar colonial vein that he'd written for the Thames TV series **Frontier** (1968).

[65] Holmes explicitly describes the 1920s characters as 'fossilised' in an interview quoted by Molesworth (*Robert Holmes* p178), going on to flippantly suggest that Major Daly has been reading his book now for '3,000 years'. While this remark may not reflect authorial intent at the time, it raises story possibilities we'll return to later. Holmes considering the Raj characters fossils may have informed his decision to put them in a display alongside a long extinct

Holmes was with the Second Battalion, Black Watch, which fought a long and hard guerrilla war behind the lines in Japanese-occupied Burma as part of a special operations group colloquially known as 'Chindits'[66]. If Holmes saw guerrilla warfare close up it's likely to have had a profound effect on him and his outlook on life. Without wanting to fall into the trap of mapping an author's life experience onto their work, one can easily imagine that period informing the black humour and sometimes brutal action in his writing. Even if Holmes was only in contact with Chindits during that period rather than fighting alongside them, the conditions they faced certainly seem to have found their way into his writing.

The jungle territories the Chindits operated in included vast swamps. Just like the Miniscope swamplands of the Drashigs these swamps released copious marsh gas[67]. Burma had rich natural gas

---

dinosaur, something that should be a fossil itself by rights. The periods for them are wrong, but they may have been displayed in the same Scope tableau thematically, perhaps as dominant lifeforms that have had their day.

[66] For more background on The Black Watch, see 'Black Watch History: Second World War – 1939-45'. I'm indebted to Paul Ford for sharing his researches into Holmes' military service online, backing up suspicions I'd been developing with solid scholarly research. The name 'Chindits' derives from Chinthe, lion-like mythical creatures whose statues guarded Burmese Buddhist temples. Is it possible Holmes' bulky statue of a 'minor Chinese deity' was actually a Chinthe? It would have such a lovely, pleasing symmetry that I'm forced to believe it wasn't.

[67] The swamp doesn't appear to be a genuine part of the Drashig home world orbiting the planet Grundle. The Drashigs vanish leaving it behind, just as the SS *Bernice* vanishes from its ocean setting when the Doctor sends the specimens home. Either the Scope lays on suitable surroundings for its captives, the Doctor

fields (now independent and renamed Myanmar, the country continues to export gas internationally). This petrochemical wealth appears to have been a major factor influencing Britain's desire to occupy and colonise the country in the 19th Century. Indeed the Burmah Oil Company, a British firm founded in 1886 (now part of BP), owed its foundation, name and wealth to Burmese gas and oil. Reclaiming control of these resources certainly motivated the British campaign against Burma's occupation by Japan during the Second World War, and it could be argued the country's petrochemical wealth has shaped much of its troubled history since.

Explosive natural gas bubbling up from underground was one symptom of the country's rich geology, but it wasn't a phenomenon limited to marshland. Methane gas was also known to erupt explosively from solid ground, usually accompanied by bursts of liquid and mud which would create cratered mounds and cones around the blowholes, sometimes described as 'mud volcanoes'[68]. I think we're deep enough into a book about **Doctor Who** now to admit this primarily interests us because of the echoes of other Holmes stories in it. The jungle warfare with explosive marsh gas in *The Deadly Assassin* (1976), the company exploiting the gas-rich swamp world of Delta Magna in *The Power of Kroll* (1978-79) and the mud bursts of Androzani Minor (a world fought

---

doesn't care much about returning a lot of small plants, fish and water, or the programme-makers needed to find an easily understood way to show the specimens departing. Choose any of the possibilities that work for you.

[68] See for example *The Physiography of Burma* by Harbans Lal Chhibber, 1933. An example of a contemporary Myanmar mud volcano can be seen at 'Minbu Mud Volcanoes' at Atlas Obscura.

over for the substances it generates underground) in *The Caves of Androzani* (1984), all seem to owe a debt to Holmes' time in Burma[69].

In looking at the development of Holmes' ideas it's also instructive to study Dicks' notes on his first storyline[70]. When Holmes writes that his alien species[71] is without weapons to turn on the Strobe, having chosen to disarm itself, Dicks writes '[c]an't have this' and

---

[69] The script description of the marsh terrain in episode 2 of *Carnival*, which calls for steaming jungle, hot geysers and mudholes seems to support the idea that Holmes was drawing on it as a location. Interestingly, in a cut sequence from the script of episode 1, scene 11 Vorg calls his home world 'Lurma', which might well be a deliberate reworking of the country's name.

[70] At this stage the storyline was entitled 'Out of the Labyrinth'. The programme entered production under the punchier title 'Peepshow', only gaining its final title after recording, when Vorg's carnival barker phrase while drumming up custom was chosen by Dicks to avoid suggestive connotations. Some online sources have claimed the title had already been used for a 1940s Ray Bradbury story. They are, however, misremembering his 1950 story 'Carnival of Madness'. It's quite possible that internal opposition to the 'Peepshow' working title and the scopophilia it implied is what caused Holmes to send Dicks a cutting advertising for erotica writers with a knowledge of fetishes on 23 November 1971, in a letter discussing the script's development. In later years Barry Letts suggested it was in response to a scripted line between Jo and the Doctor which could have been taken suggestively, but admitted that story might be apocryphal. Letts' version does seem unlikely, as Holmes' letter has him informing Dicks of his decision to have the TARDIS arrive in the hold in episode 1, which seems to indicate Dicks had not seen any scripts at this stage, let alone suggestive dialogue.

[71] At this stage the Inter Minorians are still called Lurmans.

proposes instead that the Strobe should be invulnerable to attack like the TARDIS.

Another note requests '[l]ose no weapons bit – diminishes villains'. It's quite possible Dicks had a lingering nervousness about the dramatic depiction of pacifist aliens dating back to his work as assistant script editor on *The Dominators*. While Inter Minorian hand weapons and the much bigger Eradicator do ultimately feature in the story, Holmes maintains an element of his idea in Kalik's statement that Zarb has disbanded the army.

Dicks also pushes to keep Jo imprisoned in the machine when the Doctor escapes and regains normal size. This helps maintain a personal engagement with that strand of the story for both the Doctor and viewers, and helps distribute the SS *Bernice* scenes throughout all four episodes.

Holmes had initially proposed an opening episode entirely on board the ship, with the reveal of the outside world saved for episode 2. It's Dicks' insistence ('must hook them with sci-fi **this** ep') that results in Inter Minor's appearances interspersed through episode 1.

Dicks is also keen to develop additional conflicts in Holmes' plot, which does not initially contain the palace coup subplot which ultimately drives much of Kalik's action, and he's eager to maintain constant threat to Vorg and Shirna and, by implication, to the occupants of the Scope throughout. One suggestion that Holmes doesn't directly take up is a proposal he '[m]aybe beef up alien scenes by making Pletrac Gestapo with death sentence for Vorg + Shirna – artistic in bureaucratic state.' To clarify the note, Dicks adds '[q]uicker analogy – "Pleasure is unnecessary."' In writing and performance Kalik fulfils the 'Gestapo' role Dicks proposes. Pletrac, on the other hand, remains essentially good-natured in Holmes' scripts, though, as we've seen, the accidental nature of his imprisoning the Doctor in the Scope in episode 4 is played down in production.

Another of Dicks' handwritten notes suggests the possibility of the SS *Bernice*'s native crew revolting. The idea is never developed, but the parallel this notion implies between bubbling revolution on Inter Minor and life under the British Raj does seem to be one Holmes subtly develops.

8: 'OUR PURPOSE IS TO AMUSE, SIMPLY TO AMUSE. NOTHING SERIOUS, NOTHING POLITICAL.'[72]

Once the idea of a television serial in which some of the characters are in effect within a second television programme has been arrived at, it doesn't take much of a leap of the imagination to see the programme as one offering a commentary on both TV in general and **Doctor Who** itself. Holmes, aware of his mixed adult and child audience, doesn't disappoint, delivering a serial we can choose to engage with at a number of levels[73].

We can recognise Shirna's 'blob in a snowstorm' as an echo of complaints about TV reception, and may also recognise the debate over the wisdom of providing entertainment for the Functionaries as one that has parallels with contemporary concerns about the social impact of TV, but there's also what seems to be the programme deliberately parodying itself.

Holmes will have been well aware of the formula a **Doctor Who** story required by this stage in his career – chiefly monster scares, jeopardy and repeated captures and escapes. One suspects the

---

[72] Vorg, episode 1.

[73] In *Writing for Television in the 70s*, Barry Letts expands on the production team's approach at that time: 'Nowadays we try to make **Doctor Who** as much for adults as for children. [...] it has developed to the point where nearly 60% of its viewers are over the age of fifteen.' Letts also asserts that *Carnival of Monsters* episode 1 is a good example of writing at two levels, explaining 'It is exciting for children and at the same time intriguing and amusing for adults.' (Hulke, Malcolm, *Writing for Television in the 70s*, p187.)

Miniscope allowed him to have a bit of fun with that formula, with its regularly scheduled and largely pointless monster appearances, its arbitrary tension-inducing aggrometer and its repeatedly resetting status quo.

Indeed, after reading one of Dicks' storyline notes indicating that Holmes' second plesiosaurus appearance is positioned too near to the episode 1 cliffhanger, it's easy to imagine Jo's line 'Suppose we're due for the monster bit any minute,'[74] as a direct response to it. It certainly nods as knowingly to an audience who understand the form of **Doctor Who** as Vorg's remark about how popular his most vicious monsters are with children.

One could certainly choose to interpret Vorg as a commentary on the character of the Doctor. He's an eccentric space traveller, likeable but with questionable moral authority, who doesn't understand how to operate the equipment he works with. His glamorous assistant Shirna in this reading might be seen as reflecting the Doctor's companion[75], an attractive and grounded young woman who punctures his pomposity[76].

One could suggest a similar analogue with the SS *Bernice*

---

[74] Episode 2.

[75] From episode 2, Vorg repeatedly describes Shirna as his 'assistant', a label then commonly used for what are now usually called the Doctor's 'companions'. Once Shirna is introduced to the Doctor as such in episode 4, he describes Jo as his assistant.

[76] Cheryl Hall's playing of Shirna and the way the camera emphasises her exasperated reactions to his failings hint at a concealed competence to the character that's greater than the script alone implies (for all Shirna may be framed as smarter than Vorg, she's still the one who naively sticks her finger on a live terminal for him).

characters, Major Daly and Claire, an older authoritarian male traveller who may well be a bit of a fabulist, with a younger, less hidebound female companion who teases him.

While these characters clearly mirror the leads, and it's tempting to make something of the fact that the actresses playing Shirna and Claire both auditioned for the role of Jo Grant[77], it's worth stressing these pairs of contrasting characters also exist for good dramatic reasons. The differences between them in authority and attitude create a dynamic that allows for bantering dialogue, and it's under cover of that that a great deal of exposition is introduced.

For me, this is the basic dramatic underpinning behind all the character pairs fandom has chosen to label 'Holmesian double acts' – if we're to find out what TV characters are thinking and doing, they generally need someone to talk to. It's the reason the Doctor has a companion or Sherlock Holmes has a Watson, to explain things to us and throw the lead characters into sharp relief. Robert Holmes is undeniably a particularly artful writer of dialogue that often serves actors well, but I'd maintain ultimately all three sets of duos in *Carnival of Monsters* are there to serve the story. One good example is Claire's love of repeatedly-viewed musical theatre, which is less a character note than a thematic one.

Like her repeated walks around the deck it introduces an idea of repeated action as an entertainment, and one of her two favoured plays, is one dealing with the exotic other as a spectacle. Oscar Asche's *Chu Chin Chow* was a big-budget musical comedy loosely based on 'Ali Baba and the Forty Thieves' that originally ran in

---

[77] A fact confirmed by both Cheryl Hall and Jenny McCracken on the Special Edition DVD commentaries.

London from 1916 to 1921. It's full of rich costumes and the kind of Empire-era stage Orientalism Holmes would later deploy in *The Talons of Weng-Chiang*. The Chu Chin Chow of the title is in fact an Arabian bandit masquerading as a Chinese man to con his way into a wealthy home.

Claire's second favourite play *Lady Be Good* (written by Guy Bolton, Fred Thompson and George and Ira Gershwin) opens with a pair of impoverished dancers trying to gatecrash their way to a free meal. While it's not impossible Holmes was suggesting an analogue of Vorg and Shirna with both these choices, it is more likely *Lady Be Good* was chosen as a prominent play of the 1920s with a star still recognisable in the 1970s[78].

In any case, *Chu Chin Chow* allows Andrews to express a disparaging opinion, explaining he's 'sailed into Shanghai 50 times' and knows 'what Johnny Chinaman's like.'[79] He reinforces repeated action, and introduces the disparity between the fantastical and the realistic, preparing us for the collision between the two, and flagging up the casual racism that underpins much of the story. The trick is it looks like inconsequential banter – nothing serious, nothing political.

It could also be argued that the guest duos offer contrasting takes on the Doctor and Jo and their relationship for no deeper reason than story mechanics. They're designed as characters for the Doctor and Jo to come into contact and (to some extent) conflict

---

[78] If we believe Claire's assertion that she's seen little of the world, she showed considerable devotion in seeing it four times. It opened in London on 14 April 1926 and by 3 June she's been on board the SS *Bernice* nearly four weeks.

[79] Episode 2.

with and are consequently devised to showcase specific qualities of the leads through their similarities and differences.

The populations of Inter Minor and the SS *Bernice* are not massively dissimilar: both locations feature a pair of male and female travellers, a handful of authority figures, and about six non-speaking characters who do all the work for them and mostly end up as disposable foot soldiers for the elite. The extent to which this is the writer drawing a deliberate parallel or devising drama for each recording block with similar available resources is up for debate, but Holmes definitely seems to repeatedly invite us to draw connections between the worlds.

Similarly, it may be tempting to see a joke concealed in the trio of Inter Minorian bureaucrats about a tendency of civil servants to want things in triplicate, but it's just as true that three is the bare number required dramatically to imply a tension in the alien society more subtle than that of two opposing factions of equal weight. When we have three Inter Minorians, two of whom are slightly bumbling and well-meaning, Kalik's more extreme ruthlessness and heightened xenophobia is marked out as a divergence from the norm.

Vorg, in essence, is a well-worn fictional archetype, a blustering trickster, and while the Doctor is on occasion played this way, the Pertwee era tends to present him as a far more straightforward hero. Indeed, Vorg's army background (only subliminally hinted at in his opening script description before episode 4 makes it explicit)[80] places him in a long line of military rogues from Plautus'

---

[80] As described in the scripts for episode 1, scene 1 (in *Writing for Television in the 70s* and the camera script): 'VORG IS A PERSON OF

Miles Gloriosus through to Falstaff and Sergeant Bilko.

Another way to interpret Vorg's character, and one I'm personally a little more inclined towards, is to see him as a stand-in for the writer. He's an itinerant bluffer offering entertainment for money and trying to reach a popular audience while placating the bureaucratic authorities putting obstacles in his way. He's armed primarily with a gift for colourful and persuasive language, deceptions to put off difficult deadlines, and tricks of misdirection he deploys to bamboozle onlookers. He also surprises quite late on with a military history he appears to wear lightly. Put like that, the character sounds a lot like the self-projection of a freelance writer jumping through the BBC's hoops to get a drama made.

Whether that's the case or not, Vorg is a character type Holmes seems to enjoy writing[81].

Perhaps surprisingly, study of the surviving rehearsal scripts reveals that Vorg's character is actually slightly played down on screen, with much of his more florid dialogue streamlined in the rehearsal process, almost certainly just to make the lines easier to learn and

---

DRAMATIC PRESENCE WITH FIERCE EYEBROWS WAXED TO A POINT LIKE KITCHENER'S MOUSTACHE'. In production, his warlike eyebrows gravitate to the more traditional facial level for moustache-like objects.

[81] Later rogues in the mould of Vorg include Garron in *The Ribos Operation* (1978) and Sabalom Glitz in *The Trial of a Time Lord* (1986). His stubborn freelance individuality is also displayed by Milo Clancy in *The Space Pirates* (1969) and, arguably, in harder-edged versions in the rebel Mandrel in *The Sun Makers* (1977), the gun-runner Rohm-Dutt in *The Power of Kroll* and the ruthless mercenary Stotz in *The Caves of Androzani*. As has been observed, characteristics like Vorg's are also often displayed by the Doctor.

say. Vorg's regular forelock-tugging addressing of the Inter Minorian tribunals as 'worships' began life as a stream of varying honorifics of slowly ascending absurdity. The rehearsal scripts contain a litany of alternatives which are either regularised or cut: 'your graciousness', 'sire', 'magnificence', 'lordships', 'grace', 'noble master', 'highness', 'most masterful lord', 'most gracious emperor', 'supremacy', 'imperial majesty', 'exalted highness', 'serene magnificence'[82].

This verbosity and over-effusive praise naturally calls to mind the later Holmes creations Henry Gordon Jago from *The Talons of Weng-Chiang* and Gatherer Hade from *The Sun Makers* and Holmes' characterisation of the Doctor in the courtroom in *The Trial of a Time Lord* (1986).

The officials of Inter Minor are obviously parody civil servants, one of Holmes' favoured comic targets, from the ridiculous man from the Ministry, Brownrose, in *Terror of the Autons* (1971) onwards. While the Tribunal members are all, broadly-speaking, officious and faintly incompetent, they also embody a range of lightly-sketched characteristics – Pletrac is excessively nervous, particularly of germs[83], Orum is a malleable dupe and Kalik actively malicious and conniving. Despite this, they all attempt to retain the detached impersonal tone of dispassionate officialdom. In Holmes' original storyline their names also incorporated numbers, perhaps hinting

---

[82] All forms of address Vorg uses in the rehearsal scripts.

[83] The obsessive Inter Minorian fear of alien infection which justifies their stringent quarantine procedures and isolation is an aspect of the story which is slightly submerged by the edits to episode 1, when an early scene in which Vorg explains Inter Minor's history is trimmed.

at a lack of unique identities or echoing the standard naming convention for UK government forms. They are rule books made into very grey flesh[84].

This impersonal nature is reflected in the officials' rejection of the first person singular pronoun. They almost entirely avoid the words 'me' and 'I', preferring to use 'one' when referring to themselves, or 'we' or 'us' emphasising their collective nature.

Kalik breaks this general rule the most describing an idea as 'Mine', and speaking of 'my dear brother'[85] and 'my plan', before eventually stating 'I'm sure that as commissioners of Inter Minor...' perhaps a line revealing his greater level of personal ambition[86].

Mention of Brownrose, whose name slides suspiciously close to a crude joke, reminds us Holmes' character names often do a fair bit of work in defining them, and while the names in this serial offer nothing quite so florid as that moniker, there are possible clues to

---

[84] P45 is one Holmes tips a wink to in his script for *The Sun Makers*, a story which similarly layers itself to offer moments of humour to an adult audience that their children will miss.

[85] Episode 3.

[86] Episode 4. To be scrupulously fair, this is not the hardest and fastest rule. Pletrac also transgresses, if slightly less, referring to 'my official report' on one occasion (episode 3), requesting that Functionaries 'follow me' and saying 'I will not accept this' at one point (though this line is not scripted) (episode 2). He also says 'me' in one of the cut sequences where he speaks Pidgin English (though it's almost impossible to construct a sentence in Pidgin without the word). Orum at least sticks rigidly to the 'rule' thanks to a trim to a scene in episode 3. In a cut exchange Kalik states Orum's cooperation will be required to allow Drashigs into the city. Orum replies 'Mine!' Dicks' novelisation introduces a number of additional Minorian 'I's (while also removing an 'I' from Minorian).

Holmes' thinking in the names he comes up with here. Following the famous model of Drashigs being an anagram of 'dish rags'[87], it's tempting to search for other revealing anagrams in the text. Sadly, no further obvious examples present themselves, though Pletrac's name is just one letter away from being an anagram of 'placater', which does seem apt for his character[88].

It's also possible Major Daly is so named as a play on 'daily', because he repeatedly lives through the same day; and it may even be that Tellurian is used not just as an unusual name meaning 'of the Earth' but because it has a strong suggestion of 'telly'[89]. Even the unseen Zarb, the ruler of Inter Minor, has a name with thematic echoes. While to **Doctor Who** fans it sounds like nothing so much

---

[87] Most commentary presumes the name was chosen because Holmes imagined that was probably what his low-budget monsters would look like or be made of, though in *Destroy All Monsters!* Katy Manning suggests the name was chosen because a bit of cloth would often be used as focus for actor's eyelines when reacting to monsters that weren't present in studio or on location. It's a nice story but, sadly, not one that other sources have corroborated.

[88] Anagrams are clearly a part of Holmes toolkit for generating names. *The Two Doctors* (1985), another Holmes' story with aliens who call us 'Tellurians', features the Androgum species – alien gourmands whose name is an anagram of 'gourmand'. Kalik's name could just about conceivably derive from 'kulak', a wealthy Russian peasant class the Soviet government attempted to socially engineer out of existence with collective farming in the 1920s. It's unlikely but would chime with the Russian feel of Orum's name in the original storyline, 'Grig', and the brief there that the planet is like an Iron Curtain nation opening up. I'm not personally persuaded.

[89] 'Tellurian' was used by EE 'Doc' Smith to mean 'human' in his Lensman stories, serialised in the 1930s and 1940s and published as novels in the 1950s. It is possible Holmes took the term from there.

as a giant insect from the planet Vortis, the name, when spoken aloud, actually sounds suspiciously like 'sahib', drawing another parallel between the worlds of the British Raj and Inter Minor.

The name 'Inter Minor' itself strongly suggests a small and inward-looking society[90].

---

[90] Those who find their patience taxed by Inter Minor may find the name more suggestive of 'interminable'.

9: 'JUST A LOOSE CONNECTION'[91]

This brings us neatly to some of the wider satirical targets of the serial.

One very clear resonance at the time will have been Britain's relationship with Europe. *Carnival of Monsters* began transmission on 27 January, less than four weeks after the UK officially entered the Common Market, on 1 January 1973. Obviously that hadn't been planned when the programme was being devised in 1971, but the move was clearly on the cards and was already being reflected fictionally in **Doctor Who**. *The Curse of Peladon*, from the start of 1972, and *Frontier in Space* (1973) which would follow *Carnival of Monsters* directly on transmission were both stories that dealt with isolationist worlds making contact with other species and the anxieties over what that might entail[92].

One very specific related anxiety of the 1970s that *Carnival of Monsters* tapped into beyond straightforward xenophobia was a fear of disease spread by increased international contact. Millions were known to have died worldwide in the Asian and Hong Kong flu pandemics of the late 1950s and the end of the 1960s respectively, and fear of such events recurring informed a great deal of popular science fiction of the time. **Doctor Who** writer Terry Nation, in particular, was repeatedly drawn to the theme of plague, most

---

[91] Vorg, episode 1.

[92] Coincidentally, Draconia – the world in *Frontier in Space* – has also suffered from a history of space plague. In Draconia's case the isolationism may stem more directly from the Japanese inspirations for Draconian culture, drawing on Japan's historical period of withdrawal, known as Sakoku.

famously in his TV series **Survivors** (1975-77).

Closer ties to Europe raised the specific fear of the spread of rabies, a disease absent in the UK at the time, but still present in domestic dogs in Spain and Italy, and in wild animals like foxes as close to the UK as France[93]. The UK's animal quarantine laws were strict to prevent rabies reaching Britain, and through the 1970s UK TV regularly screened Public Information Films warning of the disease's danger and advising holiday-makers against smuggling animals back into the UK[94]. It's probably in this context that the Inter Minorian tribunal's alarm at unregistered livestock reaching their world should be understood[95].

Probably the serial's most remarked-on line with clear political resonance is Orum's pronouncement about the Functionaries,

---

[93] There is by chance something of the rabid dog in the Drashigs. Their heads are built around the skulls of fox terrier dogs, their distinctive call incorporates the slowed down howls of sound designer Brian Hodgson's corgi bitch and at least one of them froths alarmingly at the mouth. Check out the raw model filming on the Special Edition DVD set for far more bubbly-mouthed Drashig action than you ever thought you'd need.

[94] A number of these anti-rabies public information films can be found online. A 1976 example may be viewed on the National Archives site and several more have been uploaded to YouTube by private individuals.

[95] In *Inside The TARDIS*, James Chapman also posits the 1968 Commonwealth Immigration Act and 1971 Immigration Act as potential influences (Chapman, James, *Inside the TARDIS: The Worlds of Doctor Who* pp95-96). Certainly, their restriction of UK residence rights available to subjects of former British colonies will have heightened general awareness of issues of racism, immigration policy and the legacy of empire, all of which have some bearing on *Carnival of Monsters*.

which Barry Letts comments on specifically in *Writing for Television in the 70s*: 'They've no sense of responsibility. Give them a hygiene chamber and they store fossil fuel in it'[96].

In its original form (along the lines of 'Give them a bath and they'd store coal in it'), it's a line with a rich political history, paraphrasing a snobbish disregard for the living conditions of workers and specifically miners that dates back to the early 20th century. It's quoted in George Orwell's *The Road to Wigan Pier* and is referred to several times in Hansard, the official record of the Houses of Parliament, though its original source remains obscure[97].

In the popular imagination, and certainly amongst **Doctor Who** fans[98], it's connected with the General Strike and this may well be the reason Holmes chose to use it. The General Strike occurred between 3 and 12 May 1926, and is seen by some commentators on the left as a key galvanising event in a struggle to democratise Britain[99]. It seems Major Daly and Claire, part of a social class many strikers had a clear grievance with and might like to see swept

---

[96] Episode 1.

[97] The earliest reference to the phrase in Hansard, where it is always used rhetorically to undermine a perceived Tory attitude, comes from Noel Billing on 7 April 1919. A 1926 reference alludes to it being a point of view that has been opposed now for 15 years. In *The Road to Wigan Pier* (1937) the phrase is already treated as 'an old saw'.

[98] The phrase originating in the General Strike has been referred to inter alia in a review of the VHS release in the fanzine *Time-Space Visualiser* and in *Doctor Who: The Complete History* volume 19.

[99] The Strike was crushed and its direct impact is hard to measure, but in popular history it's recalled as a powerful indicator of the strength of the workers.

away, have left England while the strike is ongoing. Whether this is deliberate on Holmes' part is essentially unknowable (he may simply have had a fondness for 1926 because it was the year of his birth), but again there may be more connecting his two sets of fossils than meets the eye[100].

This is not to paint Holmes as a left-wing or polemical writer. Holmes had a clear fondness for these end of Empire characters, they're from a period, class and milieu he enjoyed writing, and he consistently played down any serious intent behind his work. His personal politics are never raised in interviews, though Terrance Dicks has described himself as soft left as opposed to Malcolm Hulke's hard left[101], and has placed Holmes' politics as to the right of his own.

The situation is muddled in what is perhaps Holmes' most overtly political script – *The Sun Makers*, which combines the Doctor aiding a popular revolution against rapacious capitalism, with paraphrased Karl Marx quotations, lot of jokes about runaway inflation, liquidation, nods and winks to government forms and cash machines. Like *Carnival of Monsters*, it is operating on several levels and seems more interested in its rogues and villains than the oppressed masses. Holmes openly admitted it was partially inspired by frustration with his own dealings with the Inland Revenue. Working as both a freelancer and a salaried BBC employee during this period no doubt made his tax returns more complex than the

---

[100] Indeed the Raj is also beginning its slow dissolution by this point, as the non-cooperation movement in India gains strength through the 1920s.
[101] Cook, Benjamin, 'He Never Gives In… He's Never Cruel or Cowardly', DWM 508, February 2017.

norm and his bill harder to calculate. Despite that seemingly individualistic inspiration, one struggles to find in it any strong ideological conviction, beyond Holmes suspicion of the red tape that restrains his beloved rogues and tricksters and the hardly problematic position that people shouldn't be exploited (except possibly by rogues and tricksters). As Holmes said in relation to *The Sun Makers*:

> '...I always try to avoid plonking the moral a bit too heavily. Aside from the fact that it usually spoils the story, who am I to lecture people?'[102]

---

[102] Wicks, Matthew, 'Robert Holmes Interview', *Renegade*, issue 1, quoted in Molesworth, *Robert Holmes*, p334.

10: 'NO GOOD CAN COME FROM FRATERNISING WITH THESE INFERIOR RACES'[103]

The Inter Minorian Functionaries are clearly meant to represent a downtrodden working class, and the indication late in the story that some of them are taking industrial action by refusing to work double shifts suggests that the change of the balance in power Vorg fears is now underway on Inter Minor, but there is another analogue at work here.

The Functionaries and Officials are specifically said to be of different castes. The word carries two distinct sets of meanings referring to both race and societies based on the stratification of those groups. *Carnival of Monsters* strongly implies both meanings. Holmes' script introduces the Functionaries as squat and brutish and the Officials as tall, thin and grey, and the production carries the distinction through making the two types of alien so distinct they appear only distantly related to one another.

In effect they are different species[104].

---

[103] Kalik, episode 1.

[104] Holmes' script makes this explicit only once, in Pletrac's remark 'as members of the Official species we must all share President Zarb's concern.' The line proceeds Orum's fossil fuel line (episode 1). Dicks' novelisation clarifies the issue:

> 'The strangest thing of all about this strange world of Inter Minor was the fact that its people had been divided so long into two different social classes that they had gradually evolved into two different species.'

(Dicks, *Doctor Who and the Carnival of Monsters*, p10.)

Practicalities of production may have played a part here. In his director's commentary Barry Letts rues the crudity of the mass-produced Functionary masks and indicates the Officials were originally intended to be masked too, though with masks tailored to the individual performers. In conversation with Toby Hadoke in 2015, Terence Lodge remembers the masks being abandoned after the Tribunal actors rebelled against wearing them. The amount of dialogue given to the three Officials probably made the idea inadvisable if not unworkable, and as Lodge suggests it's likely much of their comedy would have been lost[105].

When we consider that as a racial allegory, the similarities between Inter Minor and the British Raj become more apparent. In both cases the ruling class has its manual labour undertaken by a servant class of a different ethnicity. In both cases the rulers distrust their workers and disparage them.

Andrews' remarks about Johnny Chinaman and his Lascar[106] crew who try to make a fool of him, and the casual bigotry of Major Daly ('I find the Madrassis a bit idle myself. Won't have them on the plantation,') are exactly of a kind with the Officials' othering of the Functionaries. This contrasts sharply with Daly's willingness to treat the Doctor kindly simply because of his apparent class and ethnicity. He may be a suspected stowaway but because the 'fellow's a sahib' Daly proposes they question him over drinks in the saloon like 'civilised people'[107].

---

[105] The discussion begins about 15 minutes into Hadoke's **Who's Round** podcast number 113.

[106] A word ultimately derived from Urdu, that was used to describe sailors from South East Asia or India.

[107] Episode 1.

Daly's line also economically informs us he is a plantation owner, and probably one who drives his workers hard. James Cooray Smith points out the name Madrassi was one devised to denote an Indian 'sub-race' made up of the peoples of British India's Madras province which covered most of southern India. It is a label imposed for the administrative convenience of those in control rather than one reflecting the identities of those labelled. It is an imposed construct of those in power just like Functionary or Tellurian.

Similarly Vorg's admission that he cannot tell Tellurians apart and Orum's admission that he finds their resemblance to both Lurmans and Minorians unpleasant both suggest a reluctance to treat them as thinking beings rather than monsters[108]. Vorg presumably wants to avoid emotional attachment to his 'livestock' and Orum presumably finds the similarity of 'lower' species to his own uncomfortable because it suggests a kinship he's not keen to acknowledge.

It intrigues me that most fan commentators don't seem to notice this fairly strong strand in a story that's built around fear of the other and the exploitation of sentient beings. Have we been brainwashed to look past it, like Andrews with his hatch cover?[109]

I think the key reason this theme goes largely unremarked lies in one of Holmes' greatest strengths and weaknesses as a writer.

---

[108] Episode 2.

[109] This is, of course, not universal. For example, Alec Charles' draws particular attention to *Carnival of Monsters*; grounding in British imperialism in 'The Ideology of Anachronism, Television, History and the Nature of Time', pp108-122 in the 2006 collection *Time and Relative Dissertations in Space* (ed David Butler).

Holmes is generally praised as a worldbuilder, someone who conjures up backstory and a wider context for what he shows on screen in telling details, usually evocative phrases or quirks of language that invite us to speculate further. There is perhaps less of this in *Carnival of Monsters* than in some of his other work, though President Zarb is a striking example of an important plot motivator whose presence is felt entirely through the words of others.

This skill is one that grows out of necessity. Holmes has very limited numbers of actors, extras and sets to play with and has to conjure the rest for us by other means. As a consequence he selects the pieces he uses to tell his stories economically, in a manner that plays to his interests and abilities.

Holmes' predilection for rich and often witty dialogue leads him to favour characters with erudite, arcane or engaging vocabularies. Basically, he's always likely to favour the fossils, civil servants and rogues over the ordinary workers[110].

There is a slow revolution in progress on Inter Minor, but it's largely sketched in references and its actors are simply extras given nothing to say but 'gobbledeygook'. Their struggle has less significance on screen than Vorg's coup against his unseen brother.

The same goes for the crew of the SS *Bernice*: for all the hint of insubordination in Andrews' line about the Lascars, and despite Terrance Dicks proposing a mutiny subplot, they are not the figures

---

[110] When Holmes eventually scripts a **Doctor Who** revolution more focussed on the workers, in the similarly satirically-tinged story *The Sun Makers,* he still manages to devote a great deal of screen time to rogues and civil servants.

Holmes chooses to tell the story through. Like the Functionaries they are played by extras.

A few small unscripted lines are spoken by the SS *Bernice* extras, principally 'Yes, sir' (episode 1) and agitated exclamations in combat. One unfortunate and coincidental echo of the story in production is the moment one of the Asian extras is dismissed from the production after reportedly going wild with his blank-firing gun during the Drashig attack on the SS *Bernice* hold. Keith Miller, a visitor to the set as a child, described the incident as follows '...there was one little fellow who was going berserk! He was firing at everyone except the monster, waving the gun about like a madman and jumping up and down like a thing possessed. Barry [...] wondered what on Earth the little man was up to, so they had to take him off and replace him! He was still jumping up and down when they took him away...'[111].

Decades later, Miller was asked about the event for the DVD production information subtitles and recalled Letts saying 'Oh my Lord. He's gone loco!' Am I alone in finding a curious and distressing mirroring of the Functionary who goes 'BESERK' (sic) in Holmes' episode 1 script here?

This is a story dealing with the oppressed that spends most of its screen time with the oppressors. Perhaps most damningly to modern eyes, the Doctor does not seem to take any part in standing up for the oppressed. In fact his moral ire is directed solely at Vorg for imprisoning the creatures in the Scope.

---

[111] Miller, Keith, 'Carnival of Monsters', *Doctor Who Fan Club Monthly* #14, reprinted in Cornell, Paul, ed, *Licence Denied: Rumblings from the Doctor Who Underground* (1997), pp181-82.

There are probably a few forces at work here. Firstly the series format would not have allowed the Doctor to involve himself in **working** to bring down the Raj or its alien analogue. Arguments about whether the Doctor can change established history and production practicalities essentially demanded the story be told on a smaller scale, and one that can still just about plausibly maintain it is neither political nor serious. The Scope literally becomes the underlying issue in microcosm.

Similarly, this is a story that seriously lacks women; they're outnumbered somewhere in the region of seven to one[112]. If there's a gender struggle similar to that of class and race on Inter Minor, it is not one the programme cares to dramatise. If there's no such struggle, mixing the genders of the Inter Minorian characters to demonstrate that is a complication the serial doesn't want to add. This is not a specific failing of this one story, however – the series as a whole struggles to put women on screen in this period. Their absence probably reflects an unconscious bias on the part of a largely male production team, who see adventure stories as a primarily male genre[113].

---

[112] Excluding stunt doubles there are 25 cast members, three of whom are women. If we decide to exclude extras, we're down to a cast of 11 including three women.

[113] The imbalance of male to female casting becomes even more marked during the later period of the series when Robert Holmes becomes script editor to producer Philip Hinchcliffe. As Major Daly tells Jo, 'No place for the fair sex, my dear' (episode 3).

11: 'THEY MUST BE IN THAT UPPER SECTION, VORG'[114]

I once wrote about the way 20th-century **Doctor Who** used studio depth to create suspense and menace[115]. Two of its most lauded early cliffhangers feature unknown forms from beyond the fourth wall entering the frame, the beginning of a great tradition of monster-POV shots in the series. In addition, the programme regularly exploited the image of something monstrous looming up behind a potential victim, unseen by them but obvious to us. In passing I also pointed out how rarely it uses physical height and depth to create threat, largely because of the studio challenge that creating towers and pits involves. Russell T Davies (**Doctor Who** showrunner from 2005 to 2010) went on to make exploiting this under-used vertical dimension a major part of his **Doctor Who**, building ascent and descent and the associated thrills and jeopardy into many scripts from his period on the show.

In Davies' online commentary on the **Doctor Who** episode *New Earth* (2006) he explains 'Telly does left-to-right very easily. All telly's like left-to-right – in and out of doors, cars – left-to-right, everything, and up-and-down is a real cinematic thing, I think. [...] The more up-and-down we get in **Doctor Who** the more exciting it gets, actually. Depth and height is more scary than just going right-to-left...'[116].

---

[114] Shirna, episode 3.

[115] In 'The Filipino Army's Advance on Reykjavik: Worldbuilding in Studio D and its Legacy' (*Time and Relative Dissertations in Space* pp161-75).

[116] The discussion begins at 27 minutes and 58 seconds. I'm

While his model is clearly cinematic and informed by an increased capacity to work with cranes and computer-generated imagery in a modern production environment, I suspect Davies himself would acknowledge that Robert Holmes got there first[117].

Holmes is by no means alone in his use of vertical jeopardy in **Doctor Who**. A series with so many escapes through shafts is always likely to feature a few that go up and down. A number of Terry Nation's **Doctor Who** stories feature prominent jeopardy over chasms, descents into tunnels, and climbing to escape from danger.

Although it's not made quite as apparent as it perhaps could be onscreen, the upper level of the Inter Minorian city is one restricted to the elite. This makes the rebel Functionary's ascent from the city floor level in episode 1 a direct challenge to the established social order, or as Pletrac puts it in the same episode, 'Another Functionary has dared to ascend to the higher level', a line which also highlights this appears to be an ongoing problem.

The story goes on to offer several more threats based on a transgressive change of level: we have the plesiosaurus rising out of

---

indebted to David Rolinson for pointing out how Davies' approach to upward and downward motion is based on that of the modern Hollywood blockbuster, and for his recommendation of Kristen Whissels' observations of this trend in film-making 'Tales of Upward Mobility: The New Verticality and Digital Special Effects' in Leo Braudy and Marshall Cohen's *Film Theory and Criticism: Introductory Readings* (2009).

[117] Davies has repeatedly cited Holmes as one the greats of British TV, specifically doing so beyond the world of **Doctor Who** fandom already familiar with his work when talking to Richard Johnson in his 2007 piece for the *Daily Telegraph* 'Master of the Universe'.

the ocean to panic the British Raj, and the Drashigs rising from the swamp to menace the Doctor and Jo. That's followed by the Drashigs' pursuit of the Doctor and Jo up through the Scope's circuits to burst into the SS *Bernice*. The Doctor's arrival on Inter Minor at the end of episode 3, rising up from the Scope, and the arrival of the Drashigs in episode 4 again follow that pattern.

The episode 3 cliffhanger originally would have exploited height and depth slightly differently. The Doctor would have been feeding a rope taken from the SS *Bernice* hold down the deep shaft established in the Miniscope circuits. Menaced by a Drashig, he would have tripped on the rope and fallen backwards into the shaft as the monster lunged towards him. The cliffhanger's resolution in episode 4 would have established the Doctor dangling in the shaft, still caught up in the rope, and shown the attacking Drashig falling past him to its doom down the shaft. After the sequence was dropped, a new episode 3 cliffhanger was constructed around the Doctor emerging from the Scope and collapsing.

If one wanted to be clever one might suggest each example, from Kalik's fear of the Functionaries rising up against the Inter Minorian elite onwards, is built around the fear of something perceived as unthinking and bestial rising up against a civilised society. While it's always worth bearing in mind prosaic explanations for these kinds of thematic echoes, Andy Murray very persuasively catalogues many more Holmes stories markedly featuring conflicts between worlds above and below in his essay, 'The Talons of Robert Holmes'[118]. Obviously, these may have arisen by chance or from a writer trying to give a sense of scale and varied location within a

---

[118] In *Time and Relative Dissertations in Space*, pp217-32.

story, or may even be largely constructs of our close viewing of the work decades on, but wittingly or not, this kind of construction seems to feature regularly in Holmes' **Doctor Who** work.

Perhaps the interesting thing is who the narrative chooses to focus on in this opposition, because for all the Drashigs' howl and the Functionaries' 'gobbledeygook', those down below are largely voiceless in this story[119].

---

[119] One would hope a 21st-century reimagining of *Carnival of Monsters* might also examine the looped lives of the Lascar crew, and perhaps allow the Doctor and Jo to witness the same situations repeating from two different perspectives, as outsiders to both worlds.

12: 'I MUST APOLOGISE. I'M AFRAID I DO NOT UNDERSTAND YOUR LANGUAGE.'[120]

Robert Holmes, a writer with an obvious delight in idiosyncratic speech, was clearly bothered by the established **Doctor Who** convention in which aliens all spoke terribly good English and no one ever chose to mention it.

The curiosity of this is first brought to our attention within the series during Holmes' period as script editor on the series a few years later, and a hand-waved explanation for it is offered which the series has subsequently built on[121].

He'd ignored the issue on his first script, *The Krotons*, which features English lettering and spoken English on a presumably alien world, but obviously felt the question needed addressing in a story in which two alien species largely unaware of humanity speak our language[122].

---

[120] The Doctor, episode 4.

[121] The 'Time Lord gift' of Louis Marks' *The Masque of Mandragora* (1976), which makes it seem everyone is speaking your language. Over time this is expanded on and clarified as an ability conferred by the TARDIS telepathic circuits.

[122] The Gonds could possibly be human colonists, but it seems far less likely the Krotons were, or would choose to speak English amongst themselves. His next three stories either avoid aliens (*The Space Pirates*) or have them infiltrating and invading Earth and having to communicate with human beings (*Spearhead from Space* and *Terror of the Autons*). The two stories Holmes writes following *Carnival of Monsters* also find ways to negotiate the issue. In *The Time Warrior* a translator is used to communicate with humans, and in *The Ark in Space* (1975) the main alien speaks only with the

Recalling the writing process in 1981 Holmes claimed an earlier draft of *Carnival of Monsters* attempted to comment on the problem of communication by having the Inter Minorian Pletrac address Vorg in a form of Pidgin English[123], 'lampshading'[124] the problem as blatantly as his lines about the basic similarity of alien forms highlight a second **Doctor Who** convention[125]. Holmes recalled the producer vetoing it for not being in the **Doctor Who** format, but here his memory was at fault. In fact, the two scenes using Pidgin both made it into the camera script and were only cut

---

voice of a human it has consumed mentally and physically. A short run of nine stories follow, script edited by Holmes (including two he heavily rewrites), only one of which fully avoids the problem (*The Seeds of Doom* (1976), which follows *The Ark in Space*'s model) before *The Masque of Mandragora* addresses the issue head-on.

[123] Holmes describes it as 'rather like South-Sea Pidgin English' and it does follow the construction of the Papua New Guinea Pidgin creole we now generally call 'Tok Pisin' quite closely.

[124] A useful phrase that has gained popularity in fan criticism. It's similar to the fan-identified writing gambits 'You can't fire me, I quit,' and 'A message from Fred', and refers to a production deliberately drawing attention to an issue its makers suspect audiences may have a problem with (metaphorically hanging a lampshade on it), in order to diffuse the problem without actually addressing it. Generally, it's used to gloss over anything that's too complex to explore without pausing the narrative or muddling the storytelling. Drawing attention to it is felt to send a signal to audiences that the writers know what they're doing.

[125] Holmes casually introduces a scholarly debate over whether the similarity of Lurmans, Tellurians and Inter Minorians to actors in Television Centre is significant. 'Some scientists think that their discovery refutes Valdek's theory that life in the universe is infinitely variable' (episode 2). It's another majestically cheeky 'lampshade'.

from the show when the serial's episodes were restructured in the edit[126].

It some ways the loss is regrettable. The initial sequence of mutual incomprehension is amusingly written but also deftly highlights the themes of class, race and fear of the other that quietly inform much of the serial. Vorg is angered at being treated as a savage but in turn makes the assumption the Inter Minorian is speaking his 'servant language' and that the planet's culture may still be 'feudal'.

The second, shorter sequence, has Vorg explain he and Shirna are fitted with translator diodes and essentially telling viewers they need worry no further about such matters.

These Pidgin scenes directly contrast with one where the Doctor meets a group of chickens in episode 1, in which, presuming them to be an intelligent species until the evidence contradicts him, he addresses them without condescension. This short scene is one that may have been consciously or unconsciously echoed in the Doctor's final scene in *Paradise Towers* (1987), when he doffs his hat to a metallic construction assuming it might be sentient, despite mild mockery from his companion. Like the faint similarities to *Carnival of Monsters* noted in *Enlightenment* episode 1, this may be pure coincidence. However, *Carnival of Monsters*' 1981 repeat probably makes it more likely than most Pertwee stories to have subliminally inspired elements of 1980s **Doctor Who**. The Doctor and Jo's kindness and respect towards the chickens is another

---

[126] The first Pidgin exchange survives in the early edit of episode 2 on the Special Edition DVD set. The script pages are reproduced in full in *Doctor Who: An Adventure in Space and Time* #80, p4.

elegant touch of Holmes' economy as a writer. Here we learn our lead characters have an openness towards and compassion for other creatures with contrasts with that of others. Compressed in Major Daly's short speech in which we learn he's a racially-prejudiced plantation owner is the implication these chickens will be killed for his curry. It's another microcosmic representation of livestock being treated without thought. Holmes makes his distaste at the killing of animals for food more explicit in *The Two Doctors*.

The scene also tells us the Doctor can't speak chicken[127]. It's interesting that the story, either consciously or not, also has the Doctor failing either accurately to use the linguistic codes of the British Raj or comprehend Vorg's Palare.

The Doctor's attempt at 1920s slang has him reach for the phrase '23 Skidoo' broadly, meaning to make a sudden exit, and use instead the meaningless phrase '99 Skidoo', which in the camera script clearly baffles Daly (episode 2). As scripted he says 'Eh?', but Tenniel Evans says nothing at this point on screen. If he was intending to cover the moment, the idea is thwarted by the choice of camera shots. Dicks' novel has the Doctor struggling to remember his slang but does him the service of having correctly say 23. The origin of the phrase '23 Skidoo' is tortuous, confused and largely lost, but it enjoyed a new lease of life from the 1970s after being co-opted to serve in a semi-humorous conspiracy theory

---

[127] This would seem to be an oversight of the TARDIS'. Over the years we've also seen that the TARDIS can't or won't translate Zarbi, Foamasi, an Australian Aboriginal language, a variety of Gallifreyan scripts, Mogarian, Judoon and an unknown ancient written language, and can be picky about how it deals with Welsh, French and German.

based on the number 23 popularised by the writings of Robert Anton Wilson. Those who look out for significant recurrences of the number 23s either treat the number's reappearance as a mysterious portent connected to discord, chaos and change or as fun evidence of the way actively looking for patterns tends to condition us to see them. A lot of them do both. Holmes' rehearsal script is Skidoo-free with the Doctor saying 'Perfectly ripping. Must get on old chap. Pip pip.'

Palare, Polari or Parlare, as befits an underground spoken tongue, has more than one spelling. It also has more than one history, for similar reasons. While primarily thought of now as a code allowing gay men to communicate freely during the period when homosexuality was illegal in the UK, that was just one of its subcultural uses. Its origins are disputed but the name seems to derive from Italian, from which it cribs much of its vocabulary ('parlare' is the Italian verb 'to speak'), and it appears to have become a language used by entertainers and market traders, adopting elements of other code languages as it developed[128]. While it was clearly used widely by urban gay men and by merchant seamen for the reasons we now chiefly recall, it was also used in the theatre and the circus, realms that were not exclusively homosexual, but in which gay men often found themselves more accepted than in wider society. It was almost certainly within this context that it was expected to be taken in 1973[129]. The Palare used

---

[128] A brief potted history of the language can be found in Baker, Paul, 'Polari, a Vibrant Language Born Out of Prejudice'.
[129] The website Ethnologue records carnival and circus folk as having being the primary users of parlare, while also noting its gay use.

is described as 'carnival lingo' (episode 4), building on the script playfully establishing Vorg and Shirna as members of 'Galactic Equity' (as opposed to 'British Equity', the union of the actors who'd play them) in stage directions and Vorg's showman persona.

Palare is now largely extinct. Vorg's knowledge of Palare is, therefore, slightly problematic. Like the linked assertion that he's played many a Tellurian fairground, it feels slightly at odds with the Earth having been established as in a distant galaxy. It's a curiosity that seems to arise from Holmes forgetting the finer details of the cosmos he sketched in earlier in the script. Vorg's very vague knowledge of the Daleks would certainly seem to reinforce an intended distance from our concerns. The whole speech emphasises a callousness in Vorg's nature, played down in Leslie Dwyer's performance – it seems he's as happy mixing with (and presumably fleecing) humans as he is imprisoning them as livestock.

In the end, while the Doctor can travel between linguistic groups to some degree, he doesn't truly belong in any of them. He can be briefly taken as a sahib, impersonate a fairground barker or bandy legalese with an administrative tribunal, but they're not his natural roles. It's telling that, despite him being a Lord and seeing it as his duty to uphold intergalactic law, the only one of the titles given to him that he happily accepts is 'vagabond'[130].

---

[130] Episode 4.

13: 'IT'S ONLY THE SMALL BOYS LOOKING DOWN FROM ABOVE THAT SEE THE CHANGE IN THE ENVIRONMENT'[131]

Within fan circles, *Carnival of Monsters* is often seen as a story that marks a return to the series' original format after the experiment of the Earth exile period, but it's a return that also marks a number of subtle refinements. The Doctor, although it's not yet quite apparent, can now steer (or 'programme' as he has it[132]) his TARDIS with more accuracy than we have ever previously seen. In this story, that's limited to getting the right galaxy[133], but the climax of the next story sees him set the coordinates directly for another world after telepathic contact with the Time Lords. The following story finds him accurately able to return to Earth in Jo's era, and the next finds him able to get straight to his target planet, Metebelis 3, and return to Earth in Jo's era immediately afterwards[134].

A series has been set up in which the Doctor is more of a tourist with an established base than an eternal wanderer. If we want an in-universe explanation, we can assume that the Time Lords have granted the Doctor greater understanding of his machine than he

---

[131] The Doctor, episode 1.

[132] Episode 1.

[133] Which may mean a smaller grouping of stars than we might imagine, **Doctor Who**'s use of astronomical terminology being often a little loose.

[134] *Frontier in Space, Planet of the Daleks* and *The Green Death* (all 1973). While the Doctor's ability to steer the TARDIS comes and goes hereafter he's rarely as little in command as he was in the 1960s.

ever had as either an exile or fugitive, or that he has learned more of its operating principles during his researches on Earth. One of the initial tenets of the series — that past events cannot be interfered with — has now been abandoned; it was always under stress during the early historical adventures and was first explicitly challenged in *The Time Meddler* (1965), which implied history could be changed but only with serious consequences[135]. The modified replacement position appears to be that history can be changed but that it won't have any immediate effect on our present.

The Doctor's relationship with the Time Lords and theirs with the cosmos has changed too.

We learn for the first time that the Doctor successfully petitioned them to ban Miniscopes. Although their intervention is remarked on as out of character, it's clearly in tune with their developing roles as proactive figures in the **Doctor Who** universe, rather than the aloof observers they are initially portrayed as[136]. If, as seems likely, the Doctor's anecdote about attempting to attend a Galactic peace conference in the next story dates back to before televised **Doctor Who**, it too indicates a production team picturing the Time Lords in a different way. They have become like UNIT, authority

---

[135] Truly historical **Doctor Who** stories do not survive long after it, and two of the following five have the Doctor causing famous events in history.

[136] We have already seen their isolationism begin to crumble in *The War Games* (1969) when they unpick the War Chief from all of time. Do they perform this drastic act to maintain the illusion they haven't intervened , or is just so we worry they'll do the same to all of **Doctor Who** when they pass sentence on the Doctor? Who would they be attempting to deceive by it? Outsiders or themselves?

figures who will occasionally call the Doctor in to work for them[137]. Here, their assumed moral superiority backed by an intergalactic treaty gives the Doctor a right to intervene in other cultures, and by the end of *Frontier in Space* the Doctor is treating them as allies in a fight against the Daleks[138].

This view of the Time Lords as active figures is one that will become the norm and, although the Time Lords' role in *Carnival of Monsters* appears to arise from rewrites by Terrance Dicks, Robert Holmes actively guides much of this reinvention in future years as a script editor and writer. In *The Time Warrior* the Time Lords are scathingly described as 'galactic ticket inspectors' for their role in policing history[139], and the view that a Time Lord has a duty 'to insist on justice for all species' and intervene to prevent changes to history is expressed in episode 4 of *The Masque of Mandragora* (1976), script-edited by Holmes. While the Time Lords largely maintain their stated policy of non-intervention, this is increasingly regarded as a hypocritical fig-leaf disguising covert actions favouring their interests. It's another step along the way in the

---

[137] It's a process that has already begun with their decision to exile the Doctor to Earth at a time when they judge it vulnerable to attack, and in their missions for him *in Colony in Space* (1971), *The Curse of Peladon* (though there it's merely implied) and *The Mutants* (1972).

[138] Soon, under Holmes' script supervision, they will be sending the Doctor as an agent into the Dalek past to destabilise it (*Genesis of the Daleks* (1975)), an act Russell T Davies has described as the start of the Time War between the Daleks and the Time Lords that hangs over much of the early years of 21st-century **Doctor Who**. Arguably, the end of *Frontier in Space* is where the Doctor enlists the Time Lords in a conflict he was already arguing for at his trial.

[139] *The Time Warrior* episode 3.

process of **Doctor Who** beginning to tell stories about the Doctor and his enemies, rather than stories about conflicts that the Doctor stumbles into[140].

Fannishly, it's perhaps this recreation of the Doctor as an agent of other powers that justifies his failure to act in the broader issues of injustice we see in *Carnival of Monsters*. He is now deeply enmeshed in a culture of treaties, agreements and interplanetary diplomacy that means he cannot intervene to make social change on Inter Minor revolutionary, rather than evolutionary. He is also (nominally) wedded to maintaining a past order that means he cannot sweep away the injustices of the Raj[141]. That leaves the already-banned Scope as an area in which he is empowered to act. Nothing **too** serious, nothing **too** political.

---

[140] While both still exist, and have existed ever since the Daleks set out to kill the Doctor in *The Chase* (1965), stories in which the rules of the **Doctor Who** universe and the Doctor's place within it become drivers of the narrative increase in frequency.

[141] His lack of concern about apparently negating the past disappearance of the SS *Bernice* does raise questions about why he'll allow history to change here but not generally. They're not questions the series is in a rush to answer.

14: 'THOSE THINGS WILL FOLLOW US TO THE END OF TIME!'[142]

Why do we still remember *Carnival of Monsters*? What's made this story live longer than most in both the popular and fan imaginations?

Carnival of Monsters has actually had quite a remarkable afterlife for a **Doctor Who** story with no TV sequel. Like most **Doctor Who** serials from the programme's original run, it's has been novelised, and like all complete surviving stories it's been released on VHS and DVD. Unlike most of the rest it's been released on DVD twice, partly to take advantage of advances in remastering technology and partly because of the wealth of additional surviving material. It also had a rare terrestrial TV repeat nearly nine years after its initial screening in a series of re-runs billed as **The Five Faces of Doctor Who**. This repeat occurred during a period when Equity rules[143] severely limited repeats of 'out of time' programming – television programmes that were more than five years old – making a repeat of that vintage far more of an event than it would be now[144]. The repeat ratings were surprisingly strong, with the serial drawing up to 6 million viewers, more than some of the earliest Pertwee episodes achieved on first transmission[145] and higher than 18

---

[142] Jo, episode 3.

[143] British not Galactic.

[144] Several filmed TV series had been made with cast rights bought out for a flat fee, which meant they were uniquely easy to repeat on UK television in the 70s and 80s, giving some younger viewers a slightly skewed vision of older TV.

[145] *Inferno* (1970)'s highest rated episode (episode 4) reached 6 million; its lowest rating was 4.8 million, lower than all but one of

episodes of the most recently transmitted season of contemporary **Doctor Who**[146], making it one of the most widely seen **Doctor Who** serials of the 1970s.

This repeat will certainly have cemented a fondness for the serial which was beginning to grow in organised UK fandom, due in no small part to *Doctor Who Monthly*, as *Doctor Who Magazine* was then known. The programme was selected for the 1981 repeat run for a number of reasons, though chiefly because it was four episodes long (like all the serials selected for repeat) and survived in the archives in colour. It had also been directed by Barry Letts, who retained a soft spot for the serial and was at that time **Doctor Who**'s Executive Producer[147]. Barry Letts also demonstrated considerable affection for the Drashigs as monsters[148], reusing the

---

Carnival of Monsters' repeat figures. It should be pointed out that by 1973, **Doctor Who**'s ratings had built considerably and were routinely in the range of 9 to 11 million.

[146] The ratings comparison here is perhaps one of apples and oranges. Season 18 of **Doctor Who** had been scheduled opposite **Buck Rogers in the 25th Century** (1979-81) on ITV, seeking a broadly similar audience to **Doctor Who** while BBC Two offered an alternative schedule of films and sport aimed at different audiences. The opposition for **The Five Faces of Doctor Who** on BBC Two was principally the BBC One and ITN early evening news shows.

[147] In 1981 only a small number of Jon Pertwee stories were held by the BBC in colour, and although retention rates were better for his later serials, seven of the Pertwee **Doctor Who** episodes that followed *Carnival of Monsters* were no longer held in their original PAL video format. Five of these have since been recovered.

[148] Letts is quoted describing them as 'my favourite monster of all time' (Goss, James, and Steve Tribe, *The Doctor: His Lives and Times* p77).

principles behind them to create the giant maggots of *The Green Death* (1973), and continued to experiment with puppet monsters and CSO in *Invasion of the Dinosaurs* (1974). He also ensured that the Drashigs enjoyed a horrifying fictional reputation almost on a level with Vorg's spiel for them, by featuring them as terror-inducing figures in hallucinatory sequences in both *Frontier in Space* and *Planet of the Spiders* (1974)[149].

In time, their recurrences extended beyond the show, with the first appearance of a Drashig featuring prominently in the short **Doctor Who** section of a 1986 documentary *That's Television Entertainment*, marking 50 years of BBC TV[150]. The Drashigs went on to rear their heads in further BBC documentaries including the clip show series **Boxpops** (1988-92) in 1988[151], *30 Years in the TARDIS* in 1993 and *Natural History of an Alien* in 1997[152], becoming exemplars of 'classic' **Doctor Who** monsters that

---

[149] The Drashigs appear as reused props in *Frontier in Space* and as archive film in *Planet of the Spiders*. They also reappear in flashback in episode 2 of *Death of the Doctor*, a 2010 story in the **Doctor Who** spin off series **The Sarah Jane Adventures** (2007-11). Here they appear as part of a series of images representing the past of Jo Jones (nee Grant).

[150] 1 November 1986.

[151] In a montage of **Doctor Who** clips that reused a fair number of the shots selected for *That's Television Entertainment*.

[152] The documentary looked at how we might imagine life forms had evolved in various alien environments and briefly featured clips the Drashigs alongside several other **Doctor Who** aliens, and was first shown on BBC Two on 6 July 1997 as part of a season of programmes to accompany the landing on Mars of NASA's Mars Pathfinder. Many of these clips appear to have been sourced from the montage created for **Boxpops**.

demonstrably worked well on the basis of a very brief televisual showing. Drashigs were soon making cameo appearances in the original **Doctor Who** novels that began publication in 1991, notably in Paul Cornell's *Goth Opera* (1994), which also finds room for a Miniscope, and *The Eight Doctors* (1997) by Terrance Dicks[153]. The Drashigs even spawned their own glove puppet action figure released by the company Character Options during a particularly frenzied period of niche **Doctor Who** merchandising in 2011. They are currently due to feature in a **Doctor Who** audio drama from the company Big Finish Productions in January 2019, **The Fourth Doctor Adventures**: *Planet of the Drashigs*. A lot of the Drashigs' impact in truth comes down to how effective the slow-motion film shots of them moving through the swamp and smashing through bulkheads are, and from the striking and unearthly sound effect montage Brian Hodgson created for their howl. The shots look good on clip shows and in flashback scenes in a way few other **Doctor Who** creations of that period do, meaning they remain great favourites with the children of the 1970s and beyond.

Carnival of Monsters has also lent its name to a documentary screened on BBC Two's *Doctor Who Night* in 1999[154] and to an Edinburgh Festival show and two radio sketch series from comedian Colin Hoult[155].

---

[153] There are passing references to them in several other books.

[154] The documentary features clips of many of the series' more memorable creations, but not, contrarily, the Drashigs (not even just on film).

[155] Hoult named his 2010 and 2011 follow ups to *Carnival of Monsters*, *Enemy of the World* and *Inferno,* and the Radio 4 broadcast sketch show series based on the show in 2013 and 2014,

Carnival of Monsters was also turned to as a model for a live **Doctor Who** arena show in 2010, *The Monsters are Coming!* Its influence on the presentation, which built a narrative around appearances by multiple **Doctor Who** monsters being exhibited to an audience, was made explicit within the show, with the travelling showman compere who kept these creatures in a device called a 'minimiser' being revealed to be the son of *Carnival of Monsters'* Vorg[156].

It's quite an impact for such a throwaway bit of fun.

Colin Hoult's Carnival of Monsters.
[156] The show was co-written by Gareth Roberts (whose appreciation of *Carnival of Monsters* appears towards the front of this book) with Will Brenton.

15: 'KEEPING TRACK OF THE DATE'[157]

Let's finish now with a few 'in-Universe' fannish speculations, quite definitely nothing serious and nothing political.

Firstly, there's the nagging question of how time works in this story. The Doctor arrives on the SS *Bernice* with a memory of its disappearance, an event which he appears to negate, but the story neglects to show whether he retains a memory of its loss once it's been saved.

We can posit a number of scenarios. It may be history has changed, including moments earlier in the story in which the Doctor recalled the SS *Bernice*, meaning some of what we've watched now didn't happen exactly as we saw it. It may be history has changed but that change will take time to ripple out to the Doctor.

It may be history has bifurcated and the Doctor has just generated a parallel universe in which the events he initially recalled never occurred, though if that's the case its anyone's guess which fork we're now following. It may be history will still be fulfilled as the Doctor remembers it and some terrible fate may yet befall the SS *Bernice*. Did, for example, it and the plesiosaurus both end up in their correct time zones?

Doctor Who from week to week has entertained all of these possibilities. Holmes' preferred model seems to be that history can be changed, but change takes time to work its way through. It's appears to be the situation the Doctor expects when he witnesses what he takes to be his own past death in *The Two Doctors* (1985). Certainly a belief that the past can be altered and affect the future

---

[157] The Doctor, episode 1.

underlies *Genesis of the Daleks* (1975), script edited by Holmes, and the '1980' scene in *Pyramids of Mars* (1975), a story pseudonymously rewritten by him. The Major's striking off 4 June on the calendar in his cabin is clearly meant to imply the day has been successfully navigated and time has been rewritten, but there remains room for doubt. The SS *Bernice* may not actually be back exactly when it should be, and even it is there may still be time left for disaster to strike on 4 June, even though the Major has retired to bed. This book's editor, James Cooray Smith, puts forward a good argument for a simpler solution, pointing out that the 2011 'minisode' 'Night and the Doctor: Good Night' establishes that the Doctor can remember events from more than one version of the past[158]. It could be that the Doctor's recollection of the SS *Bernice* here is a memory of events from a parallel past. This may also help explain Jo's ignorance of a comparatively recent sea mystery that had been as well known as that of the *Mary Celeste*. In her personal past it hasn't happened. Whatever the case, time appears to be in a bit of a shambles already.

Major Daly seeming to be stuck in one single day may only be the beginning of his temporal troubles – it appears he's ended up in one of the three onscreen dates in **Doctor Who** history that don't match up with our own[159]. His calendar is three days out.

---

[158] **Doctor Who**: The Complete Sixth Series DVD and Blu-ray.
[159] 'C Day', the day all the computers link up in *The War Machines* (1966), is supposed to be 16 July 1966; unfortunately the story makes the day in question a Monday when it was actually a Saturday. The production team probably should have spotted this one – 16 July 1966 was also the transmission date for episode 4 of *The War Machines*. Presumably the date had been picked to give a

We can't even easily pass this off as an artefact of a badly researched Miniscope environment, like the erroneous evening daylight and obligingly punctual plesiosaurus: the calendar is with Daly as the story ends back on Earth (though his pencil seems to have got a lot thinner as a result of his trip to the Acteon Galaxy)[160]. We can probably assume it's not still 5 June 1926 in the rest of the story, even if we choose to reject Holmes' idle suggestion Daly may have been reading the same book for 3,000 years.

This off-the-cuff remark from Holmes seems to imply he imagined some kind of time-looping occurs in the Scope in addition to whatever hypnotic effect induces the occupants to repeat their actions. It answers a few concerns about how characters negotiate rest, a whole range of bodily functions, and ageing. It also explains why Major Daly isn't absolutely legless drunk, but doesn't seem to inform Holmes' thinking for most of the story – repetition is not imposed temporally but by intellectual control, which is why the Drashigs can roam free, and the speculation that the Tellurians may have bred suggests Vorg and Shirna believe time is passing as normal within the Scope. The script regularly returns to the image

---

sense of up-to-the-minute immediacy, but a pre-existing reference to a Monday in the script wasn't tracked down and dealt with. In *The Enemy of the World* (1967-68) episode 5, a newspaper report of a disaster at sea is dated Friday 17 August 2017 when it was actually a Wednesday. Finally, Major Daly's calendar is dated Tuesday 4 June 1926 when it should be a Friday.

[160] Inter Minor is located in the Acteon Galaxy in lines cut from episode 1. Sadly, the Doctor never learns just how close (in cosmic terms) he's come to Metebelis 3. He appears to be absolutely correct in his episode 1 assertion that although he may have overshot it he is on another world in 'the Acteon group'.

of goldfish in a bowl, and one suspects the popular (if erroneous) claim that goldfish have immensely short memories is the original model for the repeated behaviour we see.

So what date is it? Lance Parkin's *Ahistory* chooses not to date the Inter Minor sequences, but we can make a few informed guesses.

The Doctor does appear confident the Miniscope seen here post-dates their banning under intergalactic law; unfortunately we've no idea when that may have been. Alternatively, the Time Lords' ban may have spread throughout all time, with them using their great powers to unpick all Miniscopes from history retrospectively (naturally, they missed one – with their great power comes exceptionally poor attention to detail). In fact, given the Miniscope's powerful defence shields, ability to scoop objects out of time and space, compress vast spaces in its interior and, quite possibly, loop time, we might well suppose it's based on Time Lord technology. Its possession of an 'Omega circuit' and compatibility with the TARDIS at the story's climax certainly reinforces the notion.

Omega is capitalised in both camera script and Dicks' novelisation, meaning that viewers who may wish to can draw a connection between this story and its televised predecessor quite easily. Obviously, we know now the Omega circuit is more likely to allude to Holmes' deleted Omegans. It's also possible Omega, the Time Lord pioneer from *The Three Doctors*, owed his name to the Omegans. Omega had been named 'Ohm' in storylines up to the end of July 1972, when Letts proposed the alternative Omega. While this was obviously long after the delivery of Holmes' scripts for *Carnival of Monsters*, Letts was still involved in the editing of the serial at the time so the 'Omega circuit' line could well have still been in his mind.

This narrows our temporal setting down to just about any period in the history of the Universe but we need not despair – we do have a couple of slightly more specific dates we might use to help us. Firstly, throwing a fresh spanner into the already cluttered works of UNIT dating, Jo describes 1926 as 'about 40 years' before her time in this story[161], so if we assume the TARDIS has travelled in space but not in time that puts us about 1966. Sadly, almost all nearly plausible UNIT dating theories would expect Jo to be living in the mid-1970s at the earliest[162].

Our only other strong temporal anchor is the Doctor's bold assertion that the plesiosaurus should have died out 130 million

---

[161] Episode 1. The kind of confusion over how long ago 1926 was might well be thought to be one more likely to occur to a writer born in 1926 writing a script in 1971 for transmission in 1973, than to a character he is writing who is at least 20 years younger. 45-year-old writers do not tend to think they're nearly 50.

[162] Dicks' novelisation, published in January 1977, tidies this up to 50 years, putting Jo's UNIT days just a year or so in the past of contemporary readers. Unfortunately, a month before, in December 1976, his novelisation of *Pyramids of Mars* had been published. This story, televised earlier in 1976, had dated the next **Doctor Who** companion's home era to 1980 on screen, but in this case Dicks chose to exclude the date entirely. It's quite possible that commendable attempts to tidy up potentially confusing details like these in the Target novelisations (the most accessible record of past **Doctor Who** stories for well over a decade) contributed to an uncertainty over the UNIT era's dating which ultimately communicated itself to the TV show's production team.

years ago[163]. Sadly this is not at all helpful because we currently believe the plesiosaur order to have died out about 65 million years ago at the end of the Cretaceous era[164]. We can't even add the extra millions of years on and assume we're that far in the future because the Doctor clearly gives the date working on the assumption he's in 1926. As we can see, the Doctor is considerably worse at sums than Jo.

If we reject a contemporary / near future / mid-1960s setting, the next most logical assumption is the future and here we have quite a bit of solid and helpful data. Although the Scope appears to be capable of plucking objects from different times and places (and ultimately returning them with the help of the TARDIS) Vorg and Shirna do not appear to be able to travel in time themselves – though they do seem to be as relaxed about travel between galaxies as the Doctor is himself[165]. Given this, we may choose to apply the arbitrary restraint that none of the Miniscope specimens

---

[163] As the Doctor very specifically says 'plesiosaurus' rather than 'plesiosaur' (episode 1), we should perhaps make the effort to be as pedantic in turn, and point out the plesiosaurus is as out of place in the Indian Ocean as it was out of time. Remains of the true plesiosaurus, which gives the plesiosaur order its name, have only ever been found in the Lyme Regis area, having been primarily discovered by the celebrated 19th-century fossil hunter, Mary Anning. I imagine the Doctor would have gone on to mention this if he'd been less busy at the time.

[164] Terrance Dicks deftly avoids being picked up by smart-alecs or having to do any proper research by changing this highly specific reference to just 'millions' in his novelisation.

[165] Made clear by Vorg's assertion he's played many a Tellurian fairground despite Earth being established earlier as in a distant galaxy.

come from their future. They certainly only refer to their specimens' past and current activities, and I fear access to future knowledge would lead to a gambler and trickster like Vorg getting in far more trouble than we see in this story. With that proviso, Vorg's present-tense reference to the Ogrons serving the Daleks leads us to conclude the story is most likely to take place at some point after we see that relationship develop. That would seem to put it no earlier than the 22nd century (if we're confident the negated and overwritten timeline of *Day of the Daleks* holds firm) or perhaps the 26th century if we trust *Frontier in Space*, the story transmitted after *Carnival of Monsters* in which the Ogrons reappear.

Now, if we accept the Doctor's assertion that that Jo was born a thousand years too early to understand the principle that keeps the Miniscope hatch plates in place we could date the serial to the late 30th century, but we do have to take into account the terrible unreliability with dates the Doctor's already demonstrated, and the fact that the Scope seems to be an alien machine. It may be a thousand years before humans have this technology, but other species may have it right now. We also know that thousands of Inter Minorian years have passed since a Great Space Plague, but this is unhelpful when we don't know the length of Inter Minorian years and can't attach this Great Space Plague to any of the other known **Doctor Who** pandemics. Given the possibilities then, we can confidently date *Carnival of Monsters* to any point in history, but most likely somewhere between the late 20th and 30th centuries.

Perhaps Vorg's way's better. I'm off to rearrange my DVD shelves by theme.

APPENDIX: 'MUCH ALIKE'[166]

This appendix briefly details the serial's principal changes from camera script to screen. The camera script ordering reflects the scene numbering rather than the order of recording.

Small changes to action or dialogue are **emboldened** in the transmission order column.

Cuts are ~~struck through~~.

A blank section in the Transmission Order column indicates no significant change from the script.

I hope you'll forgive this additional and slightly curiously formatted extra synopsis. It seemed the best way to relay the sometimes complex changes between script and screen. If seeing broadly similar events play out more as you read on induces a strange sense of déjà vu, don't be alarmed. It's quite an appropriate feeling for *Carnival of Monsters* and I think, if the story tells us anything, it's that it's worth paying attention to small details...

Camera Script	Transmission Order
EPISODE 1 TELECINE 1 EPISODE 1 OPENING TITLES	
EPISODE 1 SCENE 1 CITY Orum on the city walls above the	

---

[166] The Tellurians and the Scope's shafts are both said to be 'much alike' in episode 2.

Functionaries.	
EPISODE 2 TELECINE 2. The rocket lands.	
EPISODE 1 SCENE 1A CITY Orum and Kalik watch. Shirna, Vorg and the Scope are unloaded. A Functionary climbs the city wall, is restrained with a net and shot by Vorg. Orum and Kalik prepare to meet a nervous Shirna and Vorg.	EPISODE 1 SCENE 1A CITY Orum and Kalik watch. Shirna, Vorg and the Scope are unloaded. A Functionary climbs the city wall, **attempts to rouse his fellows with a speech and is** shot by Vorg. Orum and Kalik prepare to meet a nervous Shirna and Vorg.
EPISODE 1 SCENE 2 HOLD The TARDIS arrives; the Doctor and Jo notice the atmosphere smells wrong.	
EPISODE 1 SCENE 3 CITY Shirna and Vorg attempt to attract a crowd to view the Scope[167]. Orum and Kalik observe,	

---

[167] The script indications functionaries gathering at the 'DOOR'. Presumably of the now lost Vol-Dome.

107

awaiting Pletrac, the third of their tribunal. Shirna detects a fault in the Scope.	
EPISODE 1 SCENE 4 HOLD The Doctor maintains they should be on Metebelis 3 in the Acteon Galaxy. The Doctor realises they're in some kind of machine and tries to talk to chickens. Jo finds a crate marked Singapore and questions the Doctor's claims about the Acteon Galaxy.	EPISODE 1 SCENE 4 HOLD The Doctor maintains they should be on Metebelis 3 in the Acteon **group**. The Doctor realises they're in some kind of machine and tries to talk to chickens. Jo finds a crate marked Singapore and questions the Doctor's claims about the Acteon Galaxy[168].
TELECINE 3A SHIP The Doctor and Jo emerge onto the deck, the Doctor still feels something is wrong here. Jo suggests it's something wrong with the TARDIS. They hear Daly within the saloon and enter.	TELECINE 3A SHIP The Doctor and Jo emerge onto the deck, the Doctor still feels something is wrong here. Jo suggests it's something wrong with the TARDIS. They hear Daly within the saloon and enter.
EPISODE 1 SCENE 5 SALOON	EPISODE 1 SCENE 5 SALOON

---

[168] Pertwee slightly paraphrases the line. Manning doesn't.

Hiding in the saloon, the Doctor and Jo overhear Daly, Andrews and Claire in conversation.	Hiding in the saloon, the Doctor and Jo overhear Daly, Andrews and Claire in conversation.
While Daly snoozes and Andrews and Claire walk on deck, Jo establishes this is 1926 using Daly's book.	While Daly snoozes and Andrews and Claire walk on deck, Jo establishes this is 1926 using Daly's **newspaper**[169].
As they attempt to leave the plesiosaurus rises outside, waking Daly as Andrews and Claire return.	As they attempt to leave the plesiosaurus rises outside, waking Daly as Andrews and Claire return.
The Doctor and Jo are discovered and taken for stowaways.	The Doctor and Jo are discovered and taken for stowaways.
EPISODE 1 SCENE 6 CITY	~~EPISODE 1 SCENE 6 CITY~~
Vorg attempts to mend the Scope.	~~Vorg attempts to mend the Scope.~~
Shirna worries about the	~~Shirna worries about the~~

---

[169] Holmes has Daly's book from 1926 revealing the date in his original storyline and the prop remains a book in the camera script despite being replaced in production by a 1926 copy of the *London Evening News*. The thinking was this would more conclusively prove the date, because characters would be more likely to read an old book than an old newspaper. Daly's book continues to fulfil its other roles in the story, including symbolically marking the end of the SS *Bernice*'s capture in episode 4.

friendliness of local officials. Vorg reassures Shirna they are here at the express invitation of the president. Orum and Kalik discuss the increases in violence among the Functionaries.	~~friendliness of local officials.~~ ~~Vorg reassures Shirna they~~ ~~are here at the express~~ ~~invitation of the president.~~ ~~Orum and Kalik discuss the~~ ~~increases in violence among~~ ~~the Functionaries.~~ [170] EPISODE 1 SCENE 11 CITY Pletrac joins Orum and Kalik. They discuss the uprising on the city wall. Orum disparages the Functionaries – they would use hygiene chambers to store fossil fuel if they had them.
EPISODE 1 SCENE 7 SALOON Andrews threatens to have the Doctor and Jo put in irons if they	EPISODE 1 SCENE 7 SALOON ~~Andrews threatens to have~~ ~~the Doctor and Jo put in~~

---

[170] In the scene as written, Vorg's claim to Shirna that they've been invited by President Zarb appears to be legitimate, which makes his use of faked documents later seem curious. Shirna doesn't seem to react as if she's just discovered she's been lied to, though the lines could hint that. Reducing this subplot probably benefits the narrative, removing a point of possible confusion. This scene also establishes Inter Minor as in the Acteon system, a detail that never gets to screen. A single page extract from the 5 page scene 11 fills in for the 3 pages of scene 6 here.

don't talk. Claire and Jo protest at his bullying. Daly attempts to calm things by suggesting they talk over drinks. Andrews insists on the seriousness of matters and requests the Doctor and Jo be locked in Daly cabin until the captain can see them. As Andrews takes them away, Daly muses. The newcomers aren't how he imagines stowaways.	~~irons if they don't talk. Claire and Jo protest at his bullying.~~ Daly attempts to calm things by suggesting they talk over drinks. Andrews insists on the seriousness of matters and requests the Doctor and Jo be locked in Daly cabin until the captain can see them. ~~As Andrews takes them away, Daly muses. The newcomers aren't how he imagines stowaways.~~
EPISODE 1 SCENE 8 PASSAGEWAY The Doctor spots a strange metal panel. Andrews seems unable to see it.	
EPISODE 1 SCENE 9 CABIN Andrews locks the Doctor and Jo in. The Doctor surmises that the metal panels are not of Earth and are blocked from Andrews'	

111

consciousness. He establishes they are on a famously missing ship, the SS *Bernice*. Jo notices that the clocks have changed and the Doctor points out it is too light outside for their supposed time and location. Jo produces skeleton keys for their escape.	
NO SCENE 10 LISTED	
EPISODE 1 SCENE 11	EPISODE 2 SCENE 3 CITY
Pletrac joins Orum and Kalik. They discuss the uprising on the city wall. Orum disparages the Functionaries – they would use hygiene chambers to store fossil fuel if they had them[171].	Kalik does not understand the purpose of Vorg and Shirna's work and travel from their data discs[172].
President Zarb believes the	They explain they are entertainers. This is considered purposeless and

---

[171] After this point the scene is cut on transmission. Information given after this point that is not conveyed to the audience includes Pletrac maintaining that Functionary caste behaviour can be modified by education to some degree, but there is now an 'epidemic of anarchy and insurrection' that Zarb believes results from the lack of variety in Functionary life. The data strips in dialogue are described as data discs in stage directions. Vorg presumes Pletrac's Pidgin is his 'servant language' and speculates Inter Minor may still be feudal. The world shut itself off thousands of years ago during a Great Space Plague and is only now opening up again.

[172] The edit means these have now been acquired off screen.

Functionaries are restless because their lives lack variety. It is hoped broadening their cultural horizons will help pacify them.

This is why Vorg and Shirna have been invited here.

Pletrac says Vorg and Shirna's species is simple, good natured and trusting and good at taking orders.

Kalik suggests they could be imported to replace the Functionaries.

Pletrac requests Vorg's data strips in a form of Pidgin English.

Both men believe they are patronising a creature of lower intelligence.

Vorg is confident they'll make a killing with the Scope on Inter Minor.

He identifies the current fault with the Scope as a bit of foreign matter inside it.

subversive by a majority Tribunal vote. The Lurmans' visa application is turned down.

Vorg asks for a document of recommendation from the great Zarb to be considered. It is in fact a document from an alien wrestler of the same name.

EPISODE 1 SCENE 12 PASSAGE

The Doctor and Jo examine the metal panel in the passageway. It's a hatch cover and the Doctor believes he has equipment that can open it in the TARDIS.	
EPISODE 1 SCENE 13 SALOON Andrews, Claire and Daly are repeating their earlier conversation. The Doctor and Jo witness the repetition. The Doctor surmises they have been programmed to repeat their actions and are part of a collection. The plesiosaurus appears again and in the confusion the Doctor and Jo manage to slip off towards the hold.	
EPISODE 1 SCENE 14 HOLD The Doctor acquires the equipment needed to open the hatch. As he emerges, the hold wall opens and a giant hand reaches in, hovering menacingly over Jo and the Doctor.	EPISODE 1 SCENE 14 HOLD The Doctor acquires the equipment needed to open the hatch. As he emerges, the hold **ceiling** opens and a giant hand reaches in and picks up the TARDIS.

EPISODE 1 TELECINE 7 EPISODE 1 CLOSING CREDITS	
EPISODE 2 TELECINE 1 EPISODE 2 OPENING TITLES	
EPISODE 2 SCENE 1 HOLD. REPRISE OF EPISODE 1 SCENE 14 The Doctor and Jo hide from the hand which then plucks the TARDIS away. The hold bulkhead seals behind it. Hoping to find the TARDIS they head back to open the metal panel in the passage.	EPISODE 2 SCENE 1 HOLD. REPRISE OF EPISODE 1 SCENE 14 The hand picks up the TARDIS and the **deckhead** seals behind it. Hoping to find the TARDIS they head back to open the metal panel in the passage.
EPISODE 2 SCENE 2 CITY The Official Tribunal study Vorg and Shirna's data. They are concerned about lack of information on their machine and return to examine it. Shirna sees the officials coming over and warns Vorg just as he is removing the problem from the Scope's circuits – a tiny TARDIS. He replaces it in the Scope as the	EPISODE 2 SCENE 2 CITY ~~The Official Tribunal study Vorg and Shirna's data They are concerned about lack of information on their machine and return to examine it.~~ Shirna sees the officials coming over and warns Vorg just as he is removing the problem from the Scope's

Tribunal approaches. Pletrac again addresses Vorg in Pidgin, Vorg now explaining he and Shirna are fitted with translator diodes and so can understand his language without this. The Tribunal demands answers on the Scope's function.	circuits – a tiny TARDIS. He replaces it in the Scope as the Tribunal approaches. ~~Pletrac again addresses Vorg in Pidgin, Vorg now explaining he and Shirna are fitted with translator diodes and so can understand his language without this. The Tribunal demands answers on the Scope's function.~~
EPISODE 2 TELECINE 2 The Doctor and Jo watch Andrews and Claire repeat their deck walk, expecting the imminent return of the plesiosaurus. Jo questions why they're waiting for it and they move on..	EPISODE 2 TELECINE 2 The Doctor and Jo watch Andrews and Claire repeat their deck, expecting the imminent return of the plesiosaurus. ~~Jo questions why they're waiting for it and they move on.~~[173]
EPISODE 2 SCENE 3 CITY Kalik does not understand the purpose of Vorg and Shirna's work and travel from their data discs. They explain they are	EPISODE 2 SCENE 3 CITY Kalik asks how the Scope entertains. Vorg demonstrates, introducing the Tellurians.

---

[173] Jo's end line and the Doctor and Jo's exit are missing from both the early edit of episode 2 and the transmitted version.

entertainers. This is considered purposeless and subversive by a majority Tribunal vote. The Lurmans' visa application is turned down. Vorg asks for a document of recommendation from the great Zarb to be considered. It is in fact a document from an alien wrestler of the same name. Kalik asks how the Scope entertains. Vorg demonstrates, introducing the Tellurians.	
EPISODE 2 SCENE 4 STROBE LIMBO The Scope shows Ogrons.	
EPISODE 2 SCENE 5 CITY Vorg promises Drashigs.	
EPISODE 2 TELECINE 3 A Drashig is glimpsed sinking into the swamp.	
EPISODE 2 SCENE 6 CITY Vorg explains the creatures are real, not recorded. He switches back to the SS *Bernice*. We hear	

the plesiosaurus roar[174].	
EPISODE 2 TELECINE 4 Script has only a hand written annotation for this section: 'TK CLAIRE SCREAM ETC.'	**EPISODE 2 TELECINE 4** Claire screams; Andrews exclaims. Jo feels sympathy for the people going round in circles like goldfish in a bowl and wants to help. The Doctor says they can't help and they make a move[175].
EPISODE 2 SCENE 7 SALOON Daly imagines shooting the plesiosaurus. He catches the Doctor and Jo hoping to sneak to the hold. He clearly has no recollection of this happening before. When the Doctor says Daly will have forgotten the Doctor and Jo's names, he is impressed and	**EPISODE 2 SCENE 7 SALOON** Daly imagines shooting the plesiosaurus. He catches the Doctor and Jo hoping to sneak to the hold. He clearly has no recollection of this happening before. When the Doctor says Daly will have forgotten the Doctor and Jo's names, **he**

---

[174] The plesiosaurus roar here is added to the script in pen.

[175] The timing here is odd. The script suggests they should have moved at the end of their previous scene, which would make sense if they want to avoid activity in the saloon by sneaking down to the hold before Daly is woken. Instead they choose to go now the plesiosaurus has appeared, when detection is more likely. Without access to a script for this scene it's unclear when this slight illogicality was introduced.

asks if he's a mind reader.	**indignantly insists he's never seen them before**[176].
EPISODE 2 SCENE 8 CITY Vorg turns up the aggrometer.	
EPISODE 2 SCENE 9 SALOON On the Scope screen we see Andrews enter with the Lascars. They carry rifles. Andrews speaks to the Doctor gesturing aggressively. The Doctor steps back from him, protecting Jo.	EPISODE 2 SCENE 11 SALOON Andrew removes his **hat**, telling Claire he intends to thrash the Doctor to within an inch of his life[177].
EPISODE 2 SCENE 10 CITY Stepping away from watching the action on the Scope, Shirna insists to Vorg the Doctor and Jo are new Tellurians. Vorg suggests they've just not noticed them before. Shirna says she's seen all the Tellurians a thousand times.	EPISODE 2 SCENE 12 CITY ~~Vorg speculates the Tellurians have been breeding, but Shirna protests the new ones are fully grown. Vorg says no one knows how Tellurians reproduce and suggests they may be kept in an~~

---

[176] An approximation of Daly's new line is written in pen on the camera script, with the 'mind reader' line crossed out. Dicks' novelisation offers another approximation of the line spoken.

[177] This trim speeds the action along. In the earlier edit the scripted action of scenes 9 to 11 is retained (though scene 9 is reduced to simply Andrews shaking a finger angrily at the Doctor on the Scope screen).

	~~incubator until fully grown.~~[178] ~~Orum asks what rite the Tellurians are performing.~~ ~~Vorg explains they're about to fight.~~[179]
EPISODE 2 SCENE 11 SALOON Andrews demands the truth from the Doctor and Jo and says they're stowaways. They insist they aren't. Andrew removes his jacket, telling Claire he intends to thrash the Doctor to within an inch of his life.	EPISODE 2 SCENE 13 SALOON
EPISODE 2 SCENE 12 CITY Vorg speculates the Tellurians have been breeding, but Shirna protests the new ones are fully	EPISODE 2 TELECINE 4

---

[178] It's perhaps not surprising this section was lost if the title 'Peepshow' was considered a bit risqué. It is, however, preserved on the earlier edit for Episode 2. The title 'Peepshow' was clearly already on the way out by this point. On the unremastered version of that edit (available on the Special Edition DVD) the title can just be made out, rubbed out, on the studio clock before the opening credits.

[179] All that remains of this scene on screen is a brief cutaway to Kalik and Orum to smooth the transition from scene 11 to scene 13.

grown. Vorg says no one knows how Tellurians reproduce and suggests they may be kept in an incubator until fully grown[180]. Orum asks what rite the Tellurians are performing. Vorg explains they're about to fight.	
EPISODE 2 SCENE 13 SALOON Andrews asks the Doctor if he's still sticking to his story as they prepare to fight. He is. They box and the Doctor knocks Andrews out before the Doctor and Jo beat a hasty retreat[181].	EPISODE 2 SCENE 14 SALOON
EPISODE 2 TELECINE 4 The Doctor and Jo flee on deck.	EPISODE 2 TELECINE 5
EPISODE 2 SCENE 14 SALOON Andrews demands they're pursued.	EPISODE 2 SCENE 15 PASSAGE The Doctor and Jo enter. Seamen pursue. The Doctor

---

[180] I'd suggest that, if Vorg had worked many Tellurian fairgrounds as he later claims, he ought to have seen children and probably have got the odd hint as to how we reproduce.
[181] The stage directions have the Doctor grab his coat, adding '(AND CLOAK?)' to cover a possible costume addition.

	closes a metal door to stop a bullet, **shutting** the door while Jo attempts to open the metal floor plate. Andrews, Daly and sailors approach with rifles. The Doctor ~~grabs a pistol from a wall clip. He~~ is surrounded and the sailors are about to shoot him.
EPISODE 2 SCENE TELECINE 5 The Doctor and Jo run to a locked door as a bullet whizzes by. Above, Andrews takes aim again, and Jo and the Doctor dodge. They try another door[182].	EPISODE 2 SCENE 16 VOL-DOME MURK[183] Vorg turns down the aggrometer.
EPISODE 2 SCENE 15 PASSAGE The Doctor and Jo enter. Seamen	EPISODE 2 SCENE 17 PASSAGE

---

[182] The geography of this sequence is adapted to fit the actual ship. As filmed, Andrews gains an extra line warning the Doctor and Jo to stop or he'll fire, the Doctor gains the line 'Who's counting?' after a weary Jo asks how many times round the ship a mile is, and it's clarified that Andrews and the crew men are gaining on them with Andrews' final line 'Now we've got them. Patel!'

[183] Despite the scene heading in the script, this occurs in the standard CITY location.

pursue. The Doctor closes a metal door to stop a bullet, holding the door shut while Jo attempts to open the metal floor plate. Andrews, Daly and sailors approach with rifles. The Doctor grabs a pistol from a wall clip[184]. He is surrounded and the sailors are about to shoot him.	A whistling sound makes the crew and Daly freeze, then, observing the Doctor and Jo but seeming blissfully uninterested in them, they resume their old routine. It's made clear they have forgotten them[185].
EPISODE 2 SCENE 16 VOL-DOME MURK Vorg turns down the aggrometer.	EPISODE 2 SCENE 10 CITY Stepping away from watching the action on the Scope, Shirna insists to Vorg the Doctor and Jo are new Tellurians. ~~Vorg suggests they've just not noticed them before. Shirna says she's seen all the Tellurians a thousand times.~~
EPISODE 2 SCENE 17 PASSAGE A whistling sound makes the crew and Daly freeze, then,	EPISODE 2 SCENE 17 PASSAGE Jo opens the panel. There is

---

[184] The storyline makes clear this is intended to be a Very gun used to fire distress flares.

[185] The scene is split here to introduce some of the cut Scene 10.

observing the Doctor and Jo but seeming blissfully uninterested in them, they resume their old routine. It's made clear they have forgotten them.	a shaft below. **The Doctor goes down**[186].
Jo opens the panel. There is a shaft below. The Doctor sends her down.	
EPISODE 2 SCENE 18 SHAFT The Doctor and Jo explore the circuits beneath the SS *Bernice*. It's a futuristic machine.	
EPISODE 2 SCENE 19 CITY Pletrac returns from a higher level, having discovered Vorg's document was faked. Kalik informs him the Scope contains illegally imported animals. Pletrac orders it destroyed by Eradicator. The Scope begins to glow under bombardment from the eradicator[187].	

---

[186] The Doctor's line 'Down you go' is amended in performance to 'Down we go', and he leads instead of Jo as scripted. The novelisation follows the scripted version.
[187] This scene again refers to the Scope as STROBE in stage

EPISODE 2 SCENE 20 SHAFT The Doctor and Jo crawl through the overheating Scope.	
EPISODE 2 SCENE 21 CITY The Eradicator fails to destroy the Scope. Orum offers the comfort that the Eradicator destroys organic molecules and so the creatures in the Scope will have been destroyed at least[188]. Vorg and Shirna check the Scope for damage.	
EPISODE 2 SCENE 22 SALOON Recovering from overheating, Daly rationalises it as a result of sunspots or an atmospheric effect. Claire and Andrews propose a walk around the deck and their old routine reasserts[189].	**EPISODE 2 SCENE 23 SHAFT** The Doctor and Jo recover from overheating too. **The Doctor gives Jo his handkerchief to dab her face.** They move on looking for a way out[190].

directions and inconsistently moves between SCOPE and STROBE in camera directions.

[188] Pletrac uses the word Scope in the script; it's replaced with his more habitual 'machine' in performance.

[189] This scene is cut entirely.

[190] As performed, the physical contact between Jo and the Doctor that opens the scene with him dabbing her face is entirely removed, and a line inserted in which the Doctor instructs her to 'mop herself down' with his hanky. It's likely that a faint suggestion

EPISODE 2 SCENE 23 SHAFT	EPISODE 2 SCENE 24 CITY
The Doctor and Jo recover from overheating too, the Doctor dabbing her face with a handkerchief. They move on looking for a way out. Without realising Jo drops the Doctor's handkerchief.	The Scope shows a **Cyberman** on a fuzzy blurred screen. ~~Vorg attempts to correct the picture with his foot.~~[191] Observing at a distance, the Officials realise the animals in the Scope are not destroyed, and that they have exposed the weakness of the Eradicator, their chief piece of defence technology to possibly hostile Lurmans. Kalik fears invasion.
EPISODE 2 SCENE 24 CITY	EPISODE 2 SCENE 25 SHAFT
The Scope shows a monster on a fuzzy blurred screen. Vorg attempts to correct the picture	Walking through the circuit the Doctor and Jo recover the Doctor's handkerchief. They admit they are lost.

of impropriety the original staging might have implied, and Jon Pertwee's bad back, conspired to bring about this change. Jo still drops the handkerchief but the low-angled staging and her positioning make it hard to spot. A cutaway to the dropped handkerchief planned in the camera script does not appear on screen.

[191] Vorg kicking the Scope is a nice bit of lost business that would have reinforced its similarity to domestic TVs, then traditionally held to be best repaired at home with a heavy thump.

with his foot. Observing at distance, the Officials realise the animals in the Scope are not destroyed, and that they have exposed the weakness of the Eradicator, their chief piece of defence technology, to possibly hostile Lurmans. Kalik fears invasion, persuading Orum that Vorg and Shirna are spies. Orum wonders if the Scope is transmitting information off-world.	They decide to look for an air vent, reasoning that air will be vented outside the machine. **They look up at a noise and a** huge spiking tool spears through the shaft **vertically**. They ~~drop to the floor and~~ **step back** it stabs **a few times at the metal floor nearby** before withdrawing. Looking **up**, they see a huge eye looking in through a grille[192].
EPISODE 2 SCENE 25 SHAFT Walking through the circuit the Doctor and Jo recover the Doctor's handkerchief. They admit they are lost[193]. They decide to look for an air vent, reasoning air will be vented outside the machine. A huge spiking tool spears	EPISODE 2 SCENE 26 CITY

---

[192] As shot, the sense of the device as a screwdriver or similar doing repairs is a little lost.

[193] The handkerchief trail is the main surviving element of the Scope as labyrinth, implied in the original working title.

through the shaft horizontally. They drop to the floor and it stabs and twists above them before withdrawing. Looking back, they see a huge eye looking in through a grille.	
EPISODE 2 SCENE 26 CITY Coming away from repairing the Scope, Vorg tells Shirna he thought he saw Tellurians in the works. He is interrupted by the Tribunal hunting for a transmitter. They find the TARDIS, which regains its normal size once removed from the Scope's compression field[194]. They are alarmed and, when Shirna mentions the new Tellurians, conclude that the new object is a container in which possibly diseased Tellurians	EPISODE 2 SCENE 27 SHAFT Using a string file, the Doctor cuts his way through a metal bar holding a wall hatch like the earlier floor hatch in place. Jo offers to go through the hatch first. The Doctor says **not this time**[195] because they don't know what's beyond it. He heads through.

[194] The script has the TARDIS make 'ITS AWESOME NOISE' and expand. Sadly, it doesn't make an awesome noise on screen. Shots fired at the TARDIS by the Tribunal's hand weapons as it expands are cut from the rehearsal script, presumably to reduce the complexity of the effects sequence.

[195] A curious line change that seems to deliberately refer back to the Doctor sending Jo down the shaft first earlier, although that sequence has now been altered so he doesn't.

might find their way to Inter Minor. Vorg assures all the Scope habitats are sealed off and the Scope cannot be escaped from.	
EPISODE 2 SCENE 27 SHAFT Using a string file, the Doctor cuts his way through a metal bar holding a wall hatch like the earlier floor hatch in place. Jo offers to go through the hatch first. The Doctor says he ought to, because they don't know what's beyond it. He heads through.	EPISODE 2 SCENE 28 CAVE The Doctor enters a cave **with Jo close behind**.
EPISODE 2 SCENE 28 CAVE The Doctor enters a cave and gives Jo the OK to follow.	EPISODE 2 TELECINE 6 The Doctor and Jo leave the cave and explore an empty boggy wilderness, in which bubbles of probably flammable marsh gas bubble up from underwater. They look around[196].

---

[196] Their exploration seems better justified on paper, where it's clear their environment is one obscured by steam, rather than the empty open terrain that reaches the screen.

EPISODE 2 TELECINE (UNNUMBERED) This is covered by a handwritten note on the script 'TK DOCTOR/JO out of Cave into Marsh + away.'	EPISODE 2 SCENE 29 CITY Pletrac and Vorg are arguing about what must be done with the Scope[197]. Orum draws Kalik's attention to a flashing **and bleeping** alert on the Scope. Kalik demands to know what it is. Shirna realises it's another fault. Vorg asks her to put the circuit it's in on the screen.
EPISODE 2 SCENE 29 CITY Pletrac and Vorg are arguing about what must be done with the Scope. Orum draws Kalik's attention to a flashing alert on the Scope. Kalik demands to know what it is. Shirna realises it's another fault. Vorg asks her to put the circuit it's in on the screen.	EPISODE 2 TELECINE 6 **The Scope shows barren marshland.**
EPISODE 2 TELECINE 6	EPISODE 2 SCENE 30 CITY

---

[197] Pletrac's opening line, in which he says 'I will not accept this,' then corrects himself to say 'one will not accept this', does not appear in the script, and would appear to have been developed in rehearsal.

A steaming jungle appears on screen, with hot geysers and mudholes. Visibility is poor[198].	
EPISODE 2 SCENE 30 CITY Vorg states the Scope is working well, but Shirna reminds him the fault has still been indicated. Kalik asks to be reminded of the creatures in this habitat. Vorg reminds him they're the carnivorous Drashigs, the children's favourites... Shirna spots something on screen	**EPISODE 2 TELECINE 7** It's the Doctor and Jo **walking** through **the marsh**.
EPISODE 2 TELECINE 7 It's the Doctor and Jo emerging through steam.	**EPISODE 2 SCENE 31 CITY**
EPISODE 2 SCENE 31 CITY Shirna says Vorg has to rescue them. Vorg protests they have no chance of survival once the Drashigs get their scent. Kalik is fascinated by this.	**EPISODE 2 TELECINE 8**

---

[198] The Burmese parallels are obvious.

EPISODE 2 TELECINE 8 Feeling uneasy, Jo and Doctor decide to head back.	EPISODE 2 SCENE 32 CITY Watching, Shirna observes they'll never make it. ~~We hear a Drashig's roar.~~[199]
EPISODE 2 SCENE 32 CITY Watching, Shirna observes they'll never make it. We hear a Drashig's roar.	EPISODE 2 TELECINE 9 **We hear a Drashig's roar.** Jo and the Doctor react to the roar, perturbed. More follow and a giant Drashig bursts up out of the swamp.
EPISODE 2 TELECINE 9 Jo and the Doctor react to the roar, perturbed. More follow and a giant Drashig bursts up out of the swamp.	EPISODE 2 TELECINE 10 CLOSING CREDITS
EPISODE 2 TELECINE 10 CLOSING CREDITS	
EPISODE 3 TELECINE 1 OPENING TITLES	EPISODE 3 TELECINE 1 OPENING TITLES
EPISODE 2 REPRISE (TELECINE 1A) The Drashig looks like it's about	EPISODE 2 REPRISE (TELECINE 1A) The Drashig looks like it's

---

[199] As screened the roar is moved to the start of the following telecine sequence.

to bear down on Jo and the Doctor. He raises his flare pistol at it, though he stands no chance. Then the Drashig heads off straight past them into the mist and away. The Doctor concludes it is hunting by scent and is following their trail out to here. Jo realises it will be at the cave when they get back there. If they get back there, the Doctor suggests. Further Drashigs are heard. The Doctor and Jo move on.	about to bear down on Jo and the Doctor. ~~He raises his flare pistol at it, though he stands no chance.~~ Then the Drashig heads off straight past them ~~into the mist~~ and away. The Doctor concludes it is hunting by scent and is following their trail out to here. Jo realises it will be at the cave when they get back there. ~~If they get back there, the Doctor suggests.~~ Further Drashigs are heard. The Doctor and Jo move on.
EPISODE 3 SCENE 1 CITY Observing, the Lurmans and Inter Minorians conclude that the Tellurians stand no chance of escape. Drashigs are rapacious, unstoppable hunters known to have devoured a whole spaceship. Kalik is given pause for thought.	EPISODE 3 SCENE 1 CITY
EPISODE 3 TELECINE 2 Multiple Drashigs are seen. The	EPISODE 3 TELECINE 2 The Doctor and Jo flee.

133

Doctor and Jo flee.	Multiple Drashigs are seen[200]. **Jo becomes stuck in deep muddy water. The Doctor uses his sonic screwdriver to ignite marsh gas in front of the Drashigs. He tries to pull Jo out as the Drashigs return.**
EPISODE 3 SCENE 2 CITY Kalik asks Vorg to intervene to help the Tellurians. Vorg is reluctant but Shirna pleads with him.	
EPISODE 3 TELECINE 3 This sequence is covered in the camera script by the handwritten words: 'FILM DRASHIGS – DOCTOR/JO ESCAPE TO CAVE'	EPISODE 3 TELECINE 3 **With no more gas to ignite, the Doctor struggles to free Jo. He pulls her free just as Vorg's hand descends to distract the Drashigs. The Doctor and Jo escape to the cave.**
EPISODE 3 SCENE 3 CAVE Jo starts talking about the hand but the Doctor hasn't time. They head back into the Scope's	

[200] The initial proposed sequence is reversed. The scene's dialogue and continuation are not detailed in the camera script.

circuitry.	
EPISODE 3 SCENE 4 SHAFT The Doctor and Jo rest. They now realise they were in another miniaturised environment and this time the people above tried to help them. The Doctor realises they're in a Miniscope, devices he helped ban, and they got caught in its compression field.	
EPISODE 3 TELECINE 4 A group of Drashigs make their way into the cave.	EPISODE 3 TELECINE 4 **A group of Drashigs on the marsh.**
EPISODE 3 SCENE 5 CITY Shirna notices the Drashigs are following the Tellurians. Vorg says he should have realised – they never give up on a scent. Shirna worries they could even get out of the Scope.	
EPISODE 3 SCENE 6 SHAFT The Doctor and Jo react to a Drashig scream.	
EPISODE 3 TELECINE 5	

A Drashig head smashes through the wall into the Scope's circuits.	
EPISODE 3 SCENE 7 SHAFT The Doctor and Jo run.	
EPISODE 3 SCENE 8 CITY The Tribunal discusses what should be done with the Scope. By law, it and the specimens in it should be destroyed, but the Eradicator has failed to do that. Pletrac favours sending the Lurmans and Scope home, but Kalik argues that breaches procedure. He suggests Pletrac approach the President before acting[201].	
EPISODE 3 TELECINE 6 The Drashig heads into the circuitry.	
EPISODE 3 SCENE 9 SHAFT	

---

[201] The end of Pletrac's second line 'In that way we dispose of the entire problem,' is accidentally missed in recording when Orum comes in too early.

Jo and the Doctor flee the Drashigs[202].	
EPISODE 3 SCENE 10 CITY A flashing light on the Scope alerts Shirna, who wakes a sleeping Vorg. He dismisses it as a minor fault, but Shirna says it's probably a Drashig.	
EPISODE 3 TELECINE 7 There are no Drashigs to be seen in the marsh on screen.	
EPISODE 3 SCENE 11 CITY Shirna thinks the Drashigs are loose in the Scope. Orum and Kalik overhear.	
EPISODE 3 SCENE 12 SHAFT Jo and the Doctor flee the Drashigs[203].	
EPISODE 3 SCENE 13 CITY Orum realises Kalik knew the	

[202] Jo's opening line 'They're still following!' does not appear on transmission. An additional Drashig film cutaway appears mid-scene.
[203] The scene is listed as a MONTAGE mixing shots of Jo and the Doctor running with pre or post-recorded model shots of the Drashigs in the circuits.

Drashigs would follow the Tellurian scent. Kalik, who is unhappy with the way Zarb intends to modernise Inter Minor, plans to use this situation to lead a rebellion against him.	
EPISODE 3 SCENE 14 SHAFT The Doctor and Jo reach a chasm. The Doctor believes it will have a route out at its base. Applying lateral thinking they realise there is rope on the SS *Bernice* they can use to descend[204].	
EPISODE 3 SCENE 15 CITY Shirna wants Vorg to stop the Drashigs. He refuses to put his hand back in, and thinks once they eat the Tellurians they'll go back to their own area. Shirna suggests cutting life support but Vorg points out it	EPISODE 3 SCENE 15 CITY Shirna wants Vorg to stop the Drashigs. He refuses to put his hand back in, and thinks once they eat the Tellurians they'll go back to their own area. Shirna suggests cutting life

---

[204] The third page of this four page scene bears the words 'Rewrite Ep.3 PPP' in the top left corner. PPP was this serial's production code and this scene was written by script editor Terrance Dicks when it became clear episode 3 was under-running. Dicks retains Jo's final line 'Lateral thinking! When in doubt, go sideways!' in his novelisation.

will kill all the specimens.

Shirna wouldn't mind that. She'd feel sorry for the Tellurians because they look a lot like Lurmans, but not the other creatures.

Vorg protests, but Shirna says the Scope is rubbishy and fourth-rate and she's not surprised the distinguished Inter Minorians wouldn't give them a visa.

Vorg is surprised she finds the Minorians dignified. She qualifies 'in a grey sort of way.'

support but Vorg points out it will kill all the specimens.

~~Shirna wouldn't mind that. She'd feel sorry for the Tellurians because they look a lot like Lurmans, but not the other creatures.~~

~~Vorg protests, but Shirna says the Scope is rubbishy and fourth-rate and she's not surprised the distinguished Inter Minorians wouldn't give them a visa.~~

~~Vorg is surprised she finds the Minorians dignified. She qualifies 'in a grey sort of way.'~~

EPISODE 3 SCENE 16 HOLD

The Doctor and Jo enter via a wall plate. They find some rope but are forced to hide when Daly and Andrews enter the hold. Daly has heard the howls of the Drashigs and they've come to investigate in the forward hold. Andrews spots Jo's foot and gets

her to come out of hiding while the Doctor remains concealed. Jo is accused of being a stowaway and taken away[205].	
EPISODE 3 SCENE 17 CITY Orum queries how Zarb can be overthrown. Kalik explains that if the Drashigs escape it will be Zarb's fault for allowing aliens on Inter Minor. People will turn against him.	
EPISODE 3 SCENE 17A CITY Orum says Kalik is forgetting that even if the Drashigs escape they'll be destroyed by the Eradicator. They won't reach the city. Kalik agrees they will require Orum's aid. Orum is qualified in techni-mechanics. The implication is that he will sabotage the Eradicator. Orum protests that molecular disintegration is a specialist field.	EPISODE 3 SCENE 17A CITY Orum says Kalik is forgetting that even if the Drashigs escape they'll be destroyed by the Eradicator. They won't reach the city. ~~Kalik agrees they will require Orum's aid. Orum is qualified in techni-mechanics. The implication is that he will sabotage the Eradicator. Orum protests that molecular disintegration is a specialist~~

---

[205] One line of Daly's lines is curtailed. As scripted, he should have said 'The old briny might be all right for fish but...'

	field.
EPISODE 3 SCENE 18 SALOON Claire tries to persuade Jo to say how she got aboard. Jo pushes Claire to see if she can see any of the oddity of her situation. She falters but does not. Andrews arrives with Daly to take Jo to the captain. She is to be arrested. Jo tries fruitlessly to get Andrews and Daly to remember their previous meetings[206]. They hear a Drashig roar – it came from the forward hold[207].	EPISODE 3 SCENE 18 SALOON Claire tries to persuade Jo to say how she got aboard. Jo pushes Claire to see if she can see any of the oddity of her situation. She falters but does not.
EPISODE 3 SCENE 19 HOLD The Doctor is in the hold. A Drashig bursts in through the wall hatch. The Doctor retreats. He dodges between crates but	EPISODE 3 SCENE 19 HOLD The Doctor is in the hold. A Drashig bursts in through the wall hatch. The Doctor retreats.

---

[206] In cut lines, Andrews imagines Jo has gone mad from weeks alone in the hold and Daly wonders how Jo knew his name. She tell him they've been introduced.

[207] This scene is amended with pencil to split it in two, removing Andrews', Daly's and Jo's lines and inserting the beginning of scene 19 in their place.

falls. The Drashig smashes into the crates. Daly and Andrews enter with Lascar sailors and fire on the Drashig. The Drashig lashes out and the crew flee in disorder.	
EPISODE 3 SCENE 20 CITY The Functionary guards around the Eradicator leave it on Kalik's orders. Orum is alarmed that it's unattended. If it overheats it can go off by accident. Kalik says it won't.	**EPISODE 3 SCENE 18 SALOON** [The conclusion of the scene split earlier.] They hear a Drashig roar – it came from the forward hold.
EPISODE 3 TELECINE 8 On the deck of the SS *Bernice* the Drashig can be heard wreaking havoc. Daly, Clare and Jo and Andrews are with the captain. Andrews is shooting out of the saloon at the Drashig. There are gunshots, sailors running. Daly wants the women to go off	**EPISODE 3 SCENE 19 HOLD** [Continuation] **The Drashig advances. The Doctor falls, followed by a crate[208].** Andrews enters with Llascar sailors and Daly. They fire on the Drashig.

---

[208] As screened, the cause is unclear.

142

in a life boat. A Lascar comes running with a machine gun. Andrews knows there's something more useful than guns in the hold – dynamite!	
EPISODE 3 SCENE 21 HOLD The Doctor has been trapped by a flying crate. Andrews enters and prises the lid off a crate of dynamite.	EPISODE 3 SCENE 20
EPISODE 3 SCENE 22 Pletrac brings news that the Lurmans are to be deported on Zarb's command, to Orum and Kalik who are standing by the Eradicator. Pletrac is alarmed at the lack of Functionaries guarding it. When he discovers Kalik told them to stand down he suspends Kalik from the Tribunal.	EPISODE 3 TELECINE 8 **Activity amongst the Lascars on the deck. The captain calls down to Andrews for a Lascar to bring a gun.** **Andrews has an idea of something better – dynamite![209]**
EPISODE 3 TELECINE 9 Daly, the Lascars and the captain	EPISODE 3 SCENE 22 Pletrac brings news that the

---

[209] The first half of this scene is reworked from the scripted version, with the involvement of Claire, Jo and Daly removed. The captain is given an additional line originally scripted for Claire.

have set up the machine-gun in the saloon. The Drashig bursts out of the top of the hold[210]. Daly machine-guns it.	Lurmans are to be deported on Zarb's command, to Orum and Kalik, **just as Orum wrenches a component from the Eradicator.** Pletrac is alarmed at the lack of Functionaries guarding it. When he discovers Kalik told them to stand down he suspends Kalik from the Tribunal.
EPISODE 3 TELECINE 10 Daly and the lascars kill the Drashig[211].	EPISODE 3 TELECINE 8 [continued] Daly wants the women to go off in a life boat. A sailor **enters** with a machine-gun. **Daly takes it.**
EPISODE 3 SCENE 24 SALOON Having killed the Drashig, Daly returns with Jo and Claire to the saloon, saying that the captain will soon be with her.	EPISODE 3 TELECINE 9 The Drashig bursts out of the top of the hold. Daly machine-guns it[212].

---

[210] A separate insert.

[211] This scene does not appear in the televised version.

[212] The geography of the scene changes to make use of the locations.

EPISODE SCENE 25 HOLD	EPISODE 3 SCENE 21 HOLD
A second Drashig is coming from the Scope's circuits. Andrews lights a stick of dynamite and throws it. The Doctor protests. The dynamite explodes and the Drashig falls back down the shaft. Andrews lights a second stick, throws it out of the hold into the Scope and flees.	The Doctor **is unconscious next to a fallen** crate. Andrews enters and prises the lid off a crate of dynamite.
EPISODE 3 SCENE 26 SHAFT	EPISODE 3 SCENE 24 SALOON
The explosions have melted the metal walls. The Doctor drops into the shaft, very concerned[213].	A second Drashig **can be heard** coming from the Scope's circuits. Andrews lights a stick of dynamite and throws it. The Doctor **comes to** and protests. The dynamite explodes and the Drashig **disappears.**
EPISODE 3 SCENE 27 CITY	EPISODE 3 SCENE 25 HOLD
The Scope's power is failing, dropping towards critical, and	Andrews lights a second stick, throws it out of the

---

[213] When or how he frees himself from the fallen crates is unclear.

Vorg doesn't know how to repair it.	hold into the Scope and flees.
EPISODE 3 SCENE 28 SHAFT The Doctor is securing rope at the edge of the abyss. A Drashig roars nearby. It charges at the Doctor who steps back, tangles his foot in the rope and falls backwards as the Drashig lunges forward and falls to its death. The Doctor dangles upside-down above the abyss.	EPISODE 3 SCENE 26 SHAFT The explosions have melted the metal walls. The Doctor **looks through** into the shaft, very concerned.
EPISODE 3 TELECINE 11 CLOSING CREDITS	EPISODE 3 SCENE 27 CITY The Scope's power is failing, and Vorg doesn't know how to repair it.
	EPISODE 3 SCENE 28 SHAFT **The Doctor is securing rope to prepare his descent to the bottom of the Scope[214].**
	EPISODE 4 SCENE 2 SALOON Andrews enters and Daly offers him a drink, which he

---

[214] The remainder of this scene, which would have formed the episode 3 cliffhanger, has been cut.

	declines as he's going to walk around the deck with Claire, clicking into their old routine. Jo realises they don't remember the attack. They don't remember her – she's not a passenger. Jo asks how they know[215]. Claire, Daly and Andrews are confused. She flees. They assume she has had too much sun but as a stowaway really needs to be stopped
	EPISODE 4 SCENE 1 SHAFT The Doctor reaches the bottom of the shaft on his rope. A dead Drashig lies nearby. He discovers another metal panel in the wall[216].

---

[215] With the splitting of this scene, a few lines of Andrews, Claire and Daly trying to makes sense of what they recall are removed.

[216] A summary of this scene is inserted in pencil into Episode 4 scene 2 in the script, as 'INT. SHAFT DOCTOR DOWN SHAFT – ROPE, SEES DEAD DRASHIG'. In the rehearsal script it follows directly from the cliffhanger resolution.

	EPISODE 4 SCENE 2 (SALOON) [Continued]. Jo realises the others can't even remember the monster attack. She rushes out. Daly assumes she has a touch of the sun. Andrews points out they can't have a stowaway wandering about and they pursue her. Claire almost seems to remember something.
	EPISODE 4 SCENE 3 CITY The Scope's power is still dropping. Vorg can do nothing. Shirna screams as a tiny Doctor stumbles out of the base of the Scope and collapses.
	EPISODE 3 TELECINE 11 CLOSING CREDITS
EPISODE 4 TELECINE 1 OPENING TITLES	EPISODE 4 TELECINE 1 OPENING TITLES

EPISODE 4 REPRISE	EPISODE 4 REPRISE
The Doctor is securing rope at the edge of the abyss. A Drashig roars nearby. It charges at the Doctor, who steps back, tangles his foot in the rope and falls backwards as the Drashig lunges forward and falls to its death. The Doctor dangles above the abyss. He straightens up and climbs down after it. The Doctor reaches the bottom of the shaft on his rope. A dead Drashig lies nearby. He discovers another metal panel in the wall.	
EPISODE 4 SCENE 2 SALOON Andrews enters and Daly offers him a drink, which he declines as he's going to walk around the deck with Claire, clicking into their old routine. Jo realises they don't remember the attack. They don't remember her – she's not a passenger. Jo asks how they know. Claire, Daly and Andrews are confused. She flees. They assume she has	

149

had too much sun but as a stowaway really needs to be stopped.

EPISODE 4 SCENE 3 CITY	EPISODE 4 SCENE 3 CITY
The Scope's power is still dropping. Vorg can do nothing. Shirna screams as a tiny Doctor stumbles out the base of the Scope and collapses.	The Scope's power is still dropping. Vorg can do nothing. Shirna screams as a tiny Doctor stumbles out the base of the Scope and collapses.
He quickly grows to full size. Pletrac wants to eradicate him, but Kalik overrules him knowing, the Eradicator is sabotaged and its use requires a Tribunal vote.	He quickly grows to full size. Pletrac wants to eradicate him, but Kalik overrules him, knowing the Eradicator is sabotaged and its use requires a Tribunal vote.
Kalik gets Orum to put the missing Eradicator component in Vorg's bag to be 'discovered' in an emergency.	~~Kalik gets Orum to put the missing Eradicator component in Vorg's bag to be 'discovered' in an emergency.~~
The Doctor starts arguing with Pletrac over his authority over him, and discovers he's on Inter Minor not Metebelis 3.	The Doctor starts arguing with Pletrac over his authority over him, and discovers he's on Inter Minor not Metebelis 3.
The Doctor tells Pletrac he is in contravention of galactic law allowing the Scope on his world.	The Doctor tells Pletrac he is
The Doctor offers to overlook the whole issue if they'll allow him to	

150

rescue Jo and help the others trapped in the Scope. Vorg looks on and is convinced the Doctor is in the carnival business. Pletrac is outvoted on using the Eradicator. Vorg attempts to talk to the Doctor in Palare. He doesn't understand.[217] The Doctor discovers the Scope is close to total breakdown, he has to rescue Jo and all the other living things in the Scope urgently.	in contravention of galactic law allowing the Scope on his world. The Doctor offers to overlook the whole issue if they'll allow him to rescue Jo and help the others trapped in the Scope. Vorg looks on and is convinced the Doctor is in the carnival business. Pletrac is outvoted on using the Eradicator. Vorg attempts to talk to the Doctor in Palare. He doesn't understand. The Doctor discovers the Scope is close to total breakdown, he has to rescue Jo and all the other living things in the Scope urgently.
EPISODE 4 TELECINE 2	

---

[217] As previously discussed, the Doctor's lecture to the Tribunal in the camera script is a rewritten addition to Holmes' rehearsal scripts, and Vorg's subsequent use of Palare is a further rewrite developed during rehearsal.

Jo is hiding, while Andrews and Daly look for her.	
EPISODE 4 SCENE 4 VOL-DOME Doctor works on the Scope[218]. Kalik and Orum watch him, assuming he is attempting to rescue his fellow Tellurians because he's a social animal.	EPISODE 4 SCENE 4 VOL-DOME Doctor works on the Scope. Kalik and Orum watch him, assuming he is attempting to rescue his fellow Tellurians because he's a social animal. **Kalik gets Orum to put the missing Eradicator component in Vorg's bag to be 'discovered' in an emergency**[219].
EPISODE 4 SCENE 5 HOLD Jo looks for the Doctor, but is recaptured by Andrews.	
EPISODE 4 SCENE 6 CITY	

---

[218] The City setting is called the Vol-Dome in this scene's heading. The stage directions again call the Scope 'THE STROBE'.

[219] This incorporation of a section of scene 3 is one of the most successful re-positionings of material in the serial. The edit is undetectable if one doesn't know it's there and requires no bridging cutaways.

The Doctor works on the Scope[220]. Its base is vibrating as Drashigs reach the outer hull[221]. Vorg wants to get off Inter Minor but finds he's in strict quarantine and can go nowhere at present.	
EPISODE 4 SCENE 7 CABIN Andrews locks Jo in Major Daly's cabin. She knows the routine and sets to work with her skeleton keys as soon as he's gone.	
EPISODE 4 SCENE 8 CITY Doctor plans to go back into the Scope. He requires components from Vorg that he will link to the TARDIS to return the other Scope captives to their rightful places. Kalik and Orum are concerned about the possibility of Kalik's stage-managed disaster for Zarb	EPISODE 4 SCENE 8 CITY Doctor plans to go back into the Scope. He requires components from Vorg that he will link to the TARDIS to return the other Scope captives to their rightful places. **In another part of the City**

---

[220] Once again 'THE STROBE' in stage directions.

[221] It's not clear why falling down the shaft hasn't killed these other Drashigs following the Doctor. Given Shirna estimates that there are 20 Drashigs, it may be that a number of the more eager ones have come together to provide a mattress that protected their slower fellows as they fell.

not happening. They will have to help it along by assisting the Drashigs in their escape from the Scope.	**Kalik and Orum have been plotting something with some Functionaries. The Functionaries disperse.** Kalik and Orum are concerned about the possibility of Kalik's stage-managed disaster for Zarb not happening. They will have to help it along by assisting the Drashigs in their escape from the Scope.
EPISODE 4 SCENE 9 CABIN Jo unlocks the door and escapes.	
EPISODE 4 SCENE 10 CITY The Doctor has created a lash-up that will project him back into the Scope, but it requires Vorg to operate one control to send him in and a second to bring him out later. Pletrac wants to prevent the Doctor going anywhere, since he has come here illegally. The Doctor gets Vorg to send him in immediately. He vanishes.	

Pletrac reacts, shooting at the Doctor's lash-up. There's a small explosion. It looks like the Doctor won't be coming back.	
EPISODE 4 SCENE 11 SHAFT The Doctor appears in the circuitry.	
NO SCENE 12 LISTED	
EPISODE 4 SCENE 13 CITY Vorg tries to repair the Doctor's lash-up. Shirna helps him detect a live terminal.	
EPISODE 4 SCENE 14 HOLD Jo is back in the hold, looking for the Doctor in the Scope workings.	
EPISODE 4 SCENE 14A SHAFT She calls for him across empty circuitry.	
EPISODE 4 SCENE 14B HOLD She hears the Doctor reply, then sees him in the workings.	
EPISODE 4 SCENE 14C SHAFT They are reunited.	

EPISODE 4 SCENE 15 CITY Shirna is looking in Vorg's bag for an object he needs to repair the Doctor's lash-up. She comes across the hidden Eradicator part. Vorg is familiar with it, remembering army years. Meanwhile Kalik is working to weaken a base panel of the Scope to let the Drashigs out.	
EPISODE 4 SCENE 16 SHAFT The Doctor and Jo struggle back to where the Doctor was projected into the Scope as the life support systems fail[222].	
EPISODE 4 SCENE 17 SALOON Claire, Daly and Andrews collapse.	
EPISODE 4 SCENE 18 CITY Pletrac explains to Orum that the extradition of Vorg and Shirna can now go ahead, having been delayed by Functionaries refusing to work double shifts.	

[222] It hasn't been spelled out, but it seems the Doctor's lash-up will only project to, and abstract him from, one point.

Orum tries to stall him so Kalik has time to release the Drashigs. A Drashig roars and Kalik screams. Kalik flees an escaped Drashig[223]. Pletrac tries to use the Eradicator. It doesn't work. Kalik is eaten. Pletrac runs. Vorg takes to the Eradicator, reattaches the missing component and shoots a number of escaped Drashigs[224].	
EPISODE 4 SCENE 19 SHAFT Collapsing in the Scope circuits with Jo, the Doctor is desperate for Vorg to activate the machine for his return. He passes out.	
EPISODE 4 SCENE 20 SALOON In the Saloon everyone lies prone.	
EPISODE 4 SCENE 21 CITY	

---

[223] Stage directions have him running across the 'VOLDOME' (sic).
[224] All this action is covered on screen (if hurriedly and confusedly) apart from the Drashig eating Kalik.

After Vorg's triumph, Shirna remembers the Doctor. Vorg tries the lash-up to bring him back with little hope.	
EPISODE 4 TELECINE 4 A Drashig vanishes from the swamp.	
	The SS *Bernice* vanishes[225].
EPISODE 4 SCENE 23 SHAFT Doctor and Jo vanish.	
EPISODE 4 SCENE 24 CITY They reappear, destroying the Scope. The Doctor explains to Jo that the other captured specimens will have been sent home.	
EPISODE 4 SCENE 25 CABIN Major Daly finally finishes his book. Claire almost remembers what's happened to her. It'll be Bombay tomorrow. Daly finally crosses through 4 June on his calendar.	

---

[225] Not listed in the camera script but presumably TELECINE 5.

EPISODE 4 SCENE 26 CITY Vorg retells his act of bravery. Pletrac expresses his gratitude. The Doctor and Jo slip away as, looking for a new career, Vorg starts using his showman skills to trick Pletrac out of money. The Doctor and Jo are confident he'll do well.	
EPISODE 4 TELECINE[226] CLOSING CREDITS	

---

[226] Presumably 6.

BIBLIOGRAPHY

Books

Baker, Paul, *Polari: The Lost Language of Gay Men*. London, Routledge, 2002. ISBN 9780415261807.

Bignell, Richard, *Doctor Who on Location*. London, Reynolds and Hearn, 2001. ISBN 9781903111222.

Braudy, Leo, and Marshall Cohen, eds, *Film Theory and Criticism: Introductory Readings*. 1974. Seventh ed, New York, Oxford University Press, 2009. ISBN 9780195365627.

Britton, Piers D and Simon J Barker, *Reading Between Designs: Visual Imagery and the Generation of Meaning in the Avengers, the Prisoner, and Doctor Who*. Austin, University of Texas Press, 2003. ISBN 9780292709270.

Burk, Graeme, and Robin Smith?, *Who's 50: 50 Doctor Who Stories To Watch Before You Die – An Unofficial Companion*. Ontario, ECW Press, 2013. ISBN 9781770411661.

Butler, David, ed, *Time and Relative Dissertations in Space: Critical Perspectives on Doctor Who*. Manchester, Manchester University Press, 2007. ISBN 9780719076817.

> Charles, Alec, 'The Ideology of Anachronism: Television, History and the Nature of Time'.

> Murray, Andy, 'The Talons of Robert Holmes'.

> Potter, Ian, 'The Filipino Army's Advance on Reykjavik: World Building in Studio D and its Legacy'.

Chapman, James, *Inside the TARDIS: The Worlds of Doctor Who*.

London, IB Tauris, 2006. ISBN 9781845111632.

Chhibber, Harbans Lal, *The Physiography of Burma*. AMS Press, 1933. ISBN 9780404548087.

Cook, Lez, *British Television Drama: A History*. London, British Film Institute, 2003. ISBN 9780851708850.

Cornell, Paul, ed, *Licence Denied: Rumblings from the Doctor Who Underground*. London, Virgin Publishing, 1997. ISBN 9780753501047.

Cornell, Paul, Martin Day and Keith Topping, *Doctor Who: The Discontinuity Guide*. London, Virgin Publishing, 1995. ISBN 9780426204428.

Davies, Richard, BFI Dossier Number 20, *Boys From the Blackstuff*, London, British Film Institute, 1984.

Davies, Russell T, and Benjamin Cook, *The Writer's Tale: The Final Chapter*. London, BBC Books, 2010. ISBN 9781846078613.

Dicks, Terrance, *Doctor Who and the Carnival of Monsters*. **The Target Doctor Who Library** #8. London, WH Allen, 1977. ISBN 9780426110255.

Dicks, Terrance, *Doctor Who and the Pyramids of Mars*. **The Target Doctor Who Library** #50. London, WH Allen, 1976. ISBN 9780491020947.

Goss, James, and Steve Tribe, *The Doctor: His Lives and Times*. London, BBC Books, 2013. ISBN 9781849906364.

Howe, David J, with Tim Neal, *The Target Book: A History of the Target Doctor Who Books*. 2007. Second ed, Bromley, Telos Publishing, 2016. ISBN 9781845831141.

Howe, David J, and Stephen James Walker, *Doctor Who: The Television Companion*. London, BBC Books, 1998. ISBN 9780563405887.

Hulke, Malcolm, *Writing for Television in the 70s*. London, Adam and Charles Black, 1974. ISBN 9780713614695.

Hunter, John, *Papua New Guinea Pidgin Phrasebook*. **Lonely Planet Language Survival Kit**. Franklin, TN, Lonely Planet Publications, 1987. ISBN 9780908086900.

Letts, Barry, *Who and Me*. Fantom Films, 2009. ISBN 9781405688901.

Molesworth, Richard, *Robert Holmes: A Life in Words*. Tolworth, Telos Publishing Ltd, 2013. ISBN 9781845830915.

Niebur, Louis, *Special Sound: The Creation and Legacy of the BBC Radiophonic Workshop*. New York, Oxford University Press, 2010. ISBN 9780195368413.

Orwell, George, *The Road to Wigan Pier*. 1937. London, Penguin Classics, 2001. ISBN 9780141185293.

Parkin, Lance, and Lars Pearson, *Ahistory: An Unauthorised History of the Doctor Who Universe*. 3rd edition. Des Moines, Mad Norwegian Press, 2012. ISBN 9781935234111.

Schuster, Marc, and Tom Powers, *The Greatest Show in the Galaxy: The Discerning Fan's Guide to Doctor Who*. Jefferson NC, McFarland, 2007. ISBN 9780786432769.

Ward, Mark, *Out of the Unknown: A Guide to the Legendary BBC Series*. Birmingham, Kaleidoscope Publishing, 2004. ISBN 9781900203104.

Wilson, Robert Anton, and Robert Shea, *The Illuminatus! Trilogy*. New York, Dell, 1985. ISBN 9780440539810.

Periodicals

Doctor Who Magazine (DWM). Marvel UK, Panini, BBC, 1979-.

Cook, Benjamin, 'Halliday Inn...', DWM #321, September 2002.

Hearn, Marcus, 'Holmes on Holmes'. DWM Winter Special, 1994.

Roberts, Gareth, 'Monster Mash'. *DWM Special: The Complete Third Doctor*, September 2012.

Doctor Who: An Adventure in Space and Time #80: *Carnival of Monsters*, 1987.

Doctor Who: The Complete History volume 19 #43: *The Three Doctors, Carnival of Monsters* and *Frontier in Space*, 2017.

Radio Times Doctor Who Special. BBC Magazines, November 1973.

Roger Liminton interview.

Pohl, Frederik, 'The Tunnel Under the World'. *Galaxy Science Fiction* volume 9 #4, January 1955.

Music

Doctor Who: The Daleks. Music by Tristram Cary, Special Sound by Brian Hodgson and the BBC Radiophonic Workshop. Silva Screen, 2017. SILCD1536.

Skaro: Petrified Forest Atmosphere ('Thal Wind').

Doctor Who: Original Television Soundtrack – The 50th Anniversary

Collection 1963-2013. Silva Screen, 2014. WHO50C.

Derbyshire, Delia, and Brian Hodgson, *Doctor Who* (Delaware Version 1972).

Simpson, Dudley, Music from *Carnival of Monsters* episode 1.

Television

Boys from the Blackstuff. BBC, 1982.

Yosser's Story.

Doctor Who. BBC, 1963-.

Carnival of Monsters. Special Edition DVD, 2011.

Commentary 1, Barry Letts and Katy Manning, 2000.

Commentary 2, Toby Hadoke, Peter Halliday, Cheryl Hall, Jenny McCracken, Brian Hodgson, Terrance Dicks.

Episode 2: Early edit.

Behind the Scenes: *Looking In* extract.

Visual effects models.

Director's amended edit, 1981.

Production subtitles by Richard Molesworth.

Destroy All Monsters!

The Goodies. BBC, 1970-80.

Kinvig. London Weekend Television, 1981.

Looking In. BBC, 1972.

Out of the Unknown. BBC, 1965-71.

Tunnel Under the World, 1966.

Red Letter Day. Granada, 1976.

Amazing Stories.

The Sarah Jane Adventures. BBC, 2007-11

Death of the Doctor, 2011.

Survivors. BBC, 1975-77.

Web

BBC Doctor Who. http://www.bbc.co.uk/programmes/b006q2x0.

'Doctor Who: The Classic Series – *Carnival of Monsters*'. http://www.bbc.co.uk/doctorwho/classic/episodeguide/car nivalmonsters/. Accessed 21 November 2017.

Tennant, David, Russell T Davies and Phil Collinson, *New Earth* Commentary. http://www.bbc.co.uk/programmes/p01x64bv. Accessed 21 November 2017.

BBC Genome Project. http://genome.ch.bbc.co.uk/.

'Dr Who: Carnival of Monsters – Episode 1'. http://genome.ch.bbc.co.uk/52331946ef2e494ea59f20ad8f 757f78. Accessed 21 November 2017.

BBC Written Archives Centre. http://www.bbc.co.uk/informationandarchives/access_archives/bb c_written_archives_centre. Accessed 21 November 2017.

'Black Watch History: Second World War – 1939-45'. The Black Watch. http://www.theblackwatch.co.uk/history-and-research/black-watch-history/second-world-war/. Accessed 21 November 2017.

'Doctor Who Live'. Wikipedia. https://en.wikipedia.org/wiki/Doctor_Who_Live. Accessed 21 November 2017.

Ethnologue. 'Polari'. https://www.ethnologue.com/18/language/pld/. Accessed 21 November 2017.

Hansard Online. Early discussions of coal in baths.

http://hansard.millbanksystems.com/commons/1919/apr/7/statement-by-dr-addison#S5CV0114P0_19190407_HOC_373,

http://hansard.millbanksystems.com/commons/1926/feb/11/scottish-board-of-health - S5CV0191P0_19260211_HOC_435. Accessed 21 November 2017.

'The Tunnel Under the World'. Internet Speculative Fiction Database. http://www.isfdb.org/cgi-bin/title.cgi?45822. Accessed 21 November 2017.

'Lady Be Good'. The Guide to Musical Theatre. http://www.guidetomusicaltheatre.com/shows_l/ladybegood.htm. Accessed 21 November 2017.

'Lampshade Hanging'. TV Tropes. http://tvtropes.org/pmwiki/pmwiki.php/Main/LampshadeHanging. Accessed 21 November 2017.

'Minbu Mud Volcanoes'. Atlas Obscura.

http://www.atlasobscura.com/places/minbu-mud-volcanoes.
Accessed 21 November 2017.

'Rabies Means Death'. The National Archives: Public Information
Films.
https://www.nationalarchives.gov.uk/films/1964to1979/filmpage_
outbreak.htm. Accessed 21 November 2017.

Baker, Paul, 'Polari, a Vibrant Language Born Out of Prejudice'. *The
Guardian*, 24 May 2010. .
https://www.theguardian.com/commentisfree/2010/may/24/polar
i-language-origins. Accessed 8 January 2018.

Blumberg, Arnold T, 'Doctor Who: Carnival of Monsters Special
Edition DVD Review'. *IGN*, 2 October 2012.
http://uk.ign.com/articles/2012/10/02/doctor-who-carnival-of-
monsters-special-edition-dvd-review. Accessed 21 November 2017.

Braxton, Mark, 'Doctor Who Story Guide: *Carnival of Monsters*'.
Radio Times. http://www.radiotimes.com/news/2010-01-
20/carnival-of-monsters/. Accessed 21 November 2017.

Brown, Peter Jenson, 'Skedaddle, Skidoodle, Skidoo: The Vanishing
History and Etymology of 23, Skidoo!' Early Sports and Pop Culture
History Blog. https://esnpc.blogspot.co.uk/2015/02/skedaddle-
skidoodle-skidoo-vanishing.html. Accessed 21 November 2017.

Davis, Mary, 'Consequences of the Strike'. The Union Makes Us
Strong: TUC History Online.
http://www.unionhistory.info/generalstrike/consequences.php.
Accessed 21 November 2017.

Ford, Paul, 'Anthony Read and Bob Holmes: From Cheslyn Hay to
Gallifrey (via Walsall)'. Wyrleyblog: Local History for Great Wyrley

and Surrounding Areas. https://wyrleyblog.wordpress.com/cheslyn-hay/anthony-read-and-bob-holmes-from-cheslyn-hay-to-gallifrey-via-walsall/. Accessed 21 November 2017.

Hadoke, Toby, *Toby Hadoke's Who's Round* #113. 27 March 2015. https://www.bigfinish.com/podcasts/v/toby-hadoke-s-who-s-round-112-march-03. Accessed 21 November 2017.

Johnson, Richard, 'Master of the Universe'. *The Daily Telegraph*, 11 March 2007. http://www.telegraph.co.uk/culture/3663738/Master-of-the-universe.html. Accessed 21 November 2017.

Mandelbaum, Ken, 'DVDs: Arabian Nights'. *Broadway Buzz*, 15 July 2005. http://www.broadway.com/buzz/10843/dvds-arabian-nights/. Accessed 21 November 2017.

Scoones, Paul, '*Carnival of Monsters* VHS Review'. *TSV* #44, June 1995. http://doctorwho.org.nz/archive/tsv44/rev-carnivalofmonsters.html. Accessed 21 November 2017.

Stevens, Alan, and Fiona Moore, '32 Cool Things About '*Carnival of Monsters*'. Kaldor City. http://www.kaldorcity.com/features/articles/carnival.html. Accessed 21 November 2017.

Wilcock, Alex, '*Doctor Who and the Carnival of Monsters*'. Love and Liberty, 17 November 2011. https://loveandliberty.blogspot.co.uk/2011/11/doctor-who-and-carnival-of-monsters.html. Accessed 21 November 2017.

BIOGRAPHY

Ian Potter has written documentaries, comedy and drama for BBC radio; over a dozen audio dramas for Big Finish Productions; plays performed at the Crucible Theatre, Sheffield, Contact Theatre, Manchester, West Yorkshire Playhouse, Leeds, and Theatre at the Mill, Bradford; and several short stories. He's also written the book and lyrics for *Jungle Jeremy and the Atomic Warrior Queen of the Congo* (the first recipient of bursary funding from the Ken Hill Memorial Musical Theatre Trust), provided sound design for Big Finish Productions, the National Museum of Science and Industry and BBC radio, and been paid by US company RiffTrax to talk over old movies.

He's presented Radio 7's **Comedy Club**, appeared on Radio 4's arts show **Front Row** and worked as an archive researcher on BBC One, BBC Two and BBC Choice TV shows. For 13 years he was a television curator at the National Museum of Photography, Film and Television.

His previous factual writing includes the book, *The Rise and Rise of the Independents* (a history of UK television's indie production sector), an essay on **Doctor Who**'s production methods for Manchester University Press and a short piece for *Doctor Who Magazine*.

He's not terribly interesting but he means well.

Coming Soon

The Black Archive #17: The Impossible Planet / The Satan Pit by Simon Bucher-Jones

The Black Archive #18: Marco Polo by Dene October

The Black Archive #19: The Eleventh Hour by Jon Arnold

The Black Archive #20: Face the Raven by Sarah J Groenewegen

The Black Archive #21: Heaven Sent by Kara Dennison

The Black Archive #22: Hell Bent by Alyssa Franke

The Black Archive #23: The Curse of Fenric by Una McCormack

The Black Archive #24: The Time Warrior by Matthew Kilburn

The Black Archive #25: Doctor Who (1996) by Paul Driscoll

The Black Archive #26: The Dæmons by Matt Barber